I am dedicating this book to my Husband and our 8 resilient, talented, and caring babies. You have definitely, contributed to the woman I am TODAY. Thank you for allowing me to not only DREAM BIG, but pushing me to see it MANIFEST.

I am also dedicating this book, to ALL of the people who loved me enough to keep every assignment assigned to you regarding me. I did not understand that "It Had To Happen". You are such a necessary component to me living my BEST LIFE.

Thank you to my parents for doing whatever you did to assure my existence in the earth. I could not be who I am without you. Thank you for GIVING ME LIFE. Thank you for LIFE'S LESSONS. You are such a necessary component to me living my BEST LIFE.

Thank you to my gurrllls that have truly blessed my **whole** life. I'm most proud of the diversity in my crew. I thank you for laughing with me, listening to me, loving me and accepting me the way that I am.

I want to thank EVERYBODY THAT DECIDED TO BE A PART OF MY FIRST BOOK. YOU HAVE INSPIRED ME! I APPRECIATE YOU!

THANK YOU, GOD, FOR COVERING ME IN THIS PROCESS. IT SEEMS LIKE ADVERSITIES LINED UP TO STOP ME FROM COMPLETETING THIS BOOK. BUT GOD!!!! WE DID IT!!!!

A Note from the very FIRST reader of
Learning to Stand Tall

Have you ever wondered why you aren't further in life than you know you should be? Questioned
why it looked like other people seemed like they were living happier lives and achieving success,
while you struggle daily to keep yourself from falling apart? Learning To Stand Tall answers those
question and more. Cynthia gives away key LIFE lessons she has learned, that you can apply to your life today to achieve more joy, happiness and success. She challenges you by offering a different perspective. And sometimes making that small adjustment in your thinking, can keep you from moving forward.

The way Cynthia summarizes her life experiences into biblical based life principals, makes you
feel like you are sitting at home having coffee with a longtime friend. She reveals intimate stories
that we can all relate to because we have all been there and experienced the pains of life. The
wisdom she shares on how to overcome life's daily struggles is priceless. This book will help you dig deep into your most intimate struggles and give you the hope needed to heal and to achieve exactly what it is you are searching for.

~Margo Cirilo

Margo is so FASINATING to me. I am in awe of all the hats she wears. When I think of the song, "I'm Every Woman" I think of Margo. There isn't anything she can't do *naturally*. And here's a truth I'd like to share....
SOON THE WORLD WILL KNOW HER NAME! Get It Margo, I CHEERING YOU ON!! Thank you for supporting my Dream.

~Cynthia Essex

Table of Contents

MY JOURNEY to STANDING TALL BEGINS HERE

FOREWARD

Throughout various times in life - whether happy, sad, or indifferent. I believe that God sends at least one individual with the charm, wisdom, wit, and hilarity to navigate through those fleeting moments. Cynthia Essex, or Mrs. Essex – as she is affectionately called – is a loving mother, profound minister, and compassionate friend that has been a steady guide to going through life with a smile and a straight posture. When I was a teenager, I met Mrs. Essex at a local church. Unlike any mother, I had ever known, Mrs. Essex approached parenting with a very comical disposition. Her children have grown to be hard-working citizens, while she enjoys a valiant husband at home. Her witty conversations and ice breaking jokes were the strings that pulled many young adults like myself near her, and allowed us a safe space to be ourselves. Our conversations have always provided wisdom, understanding, and hope for a brighter tomorrow and a more meaningful today. And I have always walked away standing tall. In this book, you will find testimony after testimony of determination, love, and peace that resonate with where you are and where you are going. You will also find your dreams, your hopes, and your future waiting to be realized in each story.

Today is the day you begin your journey.

And I know that once you begin reading this masterpiece, you will also see that the best is yet to come – commit to LEARNING TO STAND TALL.

Charles Green

I have known this young man forever and his WISDOM always amazes me. Thank you for writing my FOREWORD and I am looking forward to God's plan being revealed in your life.

Keep striving for EXCELLENCE **DR. CHARLES GREEN**

~Mrs. Essex

adversity

When circumstances or situations work against you, you
face **adversity**.

Spoiler alert …….

YOU WIN EVERYTIME!

PREFACE

David was faced with adversity on many levels, yet he overcame. If David can go through the storms and overcome......SO, CAN YOU

Psalm 56 From The Message (MSG)

A David Psalm, When He Was Captured by the Philistines in Gath

56 ¹⁻⁴ Take my side, God—I'm getting kicked around,
   stomped on every day.
Not a day goes by
   but somebody beats me up;
They make it their duty
   to beat me up.
When I get really afraid
   I come to you in trust.
I'm proud to praise God;
   fearless now, I trust in God.
   What can mere mortals do?
⁵⁻⁶ They don't let up—
   they smear my reputation
   and huddle to plot my collapse.
They gang up,
   sneak together through the alleys
To take me by surprise,
   wait their chance to get me.

7 Pay them back in evil!
   Get angry, God!
   Down with these people!
8 You've kept track of my every toss and turn
   through the sleepless nights,
Each tear entered in your ledger,
   each ache written in your book.
9 If my enemies run away,
   turn tail when I yell at them,
Then I'll know
   that God is on my side.
10-11 I'm proud to praise God,
   proud to praise GOD.
Fearless now, I trust in God;
   what can mere mortals do to me?
12-13 God, you did everything you promised,
   and I'm thanking you with all my heart.
You pulled me from the brink of death,
   my feet from the cliff-edge of doom.
Now I stroll at leisure with God
   in the sunlit fields of life.

I KNOW YOU NOT STILL SITTING DOWN!!
GO AHEAD AND RUN I'LL WAIT

(Yes, I'm Yelling and Running)

Introduction

Life and Adversity can seem to be the best of friends sometimes. But you can't stop living. The world is committed to sending us messages to feel smaller than we were created to be. We live in an age where others have unlimited access to our lives and to our minds. And if we are not careful those subtle messages can cause internal conflict and external extremes. NEVERTHELESS, you must FACE IT (adversity) and If you can win the battle within, what they say won't matter.

If you can take the time to create your "DEFINING WHY'S" (your reasoning for whatever lasting change, you desire) abandoning YOU will never be an option. I want you to know that it won't always be easy, but anything that comes easy, will leave easy. I want you to know that giving birth is painful but worth it. I want you to make the commitment to yourself. I want you to feel the fear and do it anyway! DECIDE NOW TO ENJOY THE RIDE!

See yourself driving to the place you want to go and stay on that road......**NO MATTER WHAT!** You may have a couple of storms, some car repairs, some unexpected construction zones…. BUT STAY ON THE ROAD! Only you can DO WHAT YOU DO, THE WAY YOU DO IT! THE WORLD NEEDS YOU, SO GET IN THE CAR AND START DRIVING TO THE PLACE WHERE YOU CAN STAND THE TALLEST. YOU'LL HAVE NO REGRETS BECAUSE THE VIEW IS AMAZING.

NEVER FORGET THE NEW VIEW HAS NEW RULES

Join me on this journey exploring the how's in LEARNING TO STAND TALL in the FACE of LIFE'S ADVERSITIES. We know that they are coming, SO LET'S GET INTO POSITION!

STAND TALL because IT'S GOOD FOR YOUR POSTURE

Have you ever had
life hurt you so
bad, that it
changed your
posture?

You go from
Standing to sitting,
from sitting to laying
and from laying
STRAIGHT TO A
FETALPOSITION?

Don't Allow Your LOCATION to be YOUR LIMITATION!

Well I have. I have had times in my life where I did not know what to do. It didn't seem like life could get any worse, BUT do you know your worst is someone else's BETTER.

Let's be honest Life happens, **no one escapes** it and it can throw some mean curve balls. BUT you are equipped to handle them. No matter what the balls have written on them, when they are thrown at you, get into position, YOU can handle it!! Please recognize that your worst days will look like a honeymoon compared to someone's else's worst days. How many times have you been watching TV and you see a news story that's devastating and you immediately think "that's more than I think I could handle? And in that moment your heart goes out to whomever has been affected by it. In that moment, YOU don't quite understand how they can go on…. BUT THEY DO! It's because what they needed to survive it, was already inside of them. The people they needed to meet were already placed in their path, they just needed to keep standing and keep BELIEVING, that a better day was on its way.

We don't get to choose when or where the pain will show up. We don't get to choose who or what inflicts that pain upon us. However, what we do get to choose is how we deal with it. Your attitude about the pain, will be key in your progress through it.

How we choose to deal with anything that tries to interrupt our lives is so important. You can get revenge (which isn't the smartest thing to do…just TRUST me on this one). Or at some point you can operate in compassion (assuming they just didn't know any better). Purposely moving on doesn't excuse the person or situation that hurt you, it releases you. I'm not at all suggesting that you let people mistreat you and walk over you or that your pain posture isn't valid. I am saying, you must choose a HIGHER THOUGHT and or ROAD. Your response can take you from being a victim to VICTOR.

I am convinced that life is 10% what happens to me and 90% of how I react to it. And so, it is with you… we are in charge of our Attitudes.
                                                          ~Charles R. Swindoll

Let the tears flow If you must

They have been counted and they are being cared for.

Not one

has been wasted.

You HAVEN'T given YOUSELF enough CREDIT

You did the BEST you could, with What You had

Have you ever made
a DECISION that
seemed to follow
you the rest of
your LIFE?

You go from standing
To shrinking
EVERYTIME
Your Past Collides
with your Present

Life is life AND YOU are not perfect, just like pain, you can't escape the whispers of what seems to be a *bad* decision. We try to make the best decisions; with the information, we have at the time. Those decisions are also affected by your positioning in life at the time of the decision.

I remember the day, that the heaviness of being a teen mom came crashing in on me. It wasn't a time of celebration, picture taking or baby shower planning. I was pregnant, confused and scared. Today it would be a Facebook post with 3 shoes, some paperclips, a good ole riddle or some other GRAND announcement. This wasn't that, this was the keep your head low, you should be ashamed of yourself kind of pregnancy. I don't know what was more devastating the FACT that everyone would know that I had "did it" or facing the people who had a higher expectation of me. Either way I kept my head down and I walked in my shame.

Back in those days, you know when dinosaurs walked the earth, the older women talked boldly to your face, and most of those conversations were light years ahead of my understanding. Things like "you ain't got a pot to piss in or a window to throw it out of" .... hmmmm I THOUGHT to myself (because that was the best way to stay alive...you bet not talk back) who's pissing in pots and why are they throwing it out the window.... I DIGRESS (it simply meant you have NOTHING). What wasn't misunderstood was the barrage of negative words spoken. Those words had creative powers, they had the power to build me up or tear me down. WORDS stick to you and you never forget **WHO** said it and **HOW** those words made you feel (and I'm sure they weren't intentionally attempting to reduce my already low self-esteem; I'm sure, they just didn't know any better). Let's be honest as a teen I was naïve and clueless about what was next.......

My next would include facing family members, siblings, teachers, and classmates. Thank God there was no Facebook or Social Media at this time in my life. For most of my pregnancy I felt shame, embarrassment and branded as "one of those girls". I felt like the future I often dreamed about in my head was gone. It just wasn't supposed to be like this. I FELT like I was being judged EVERYWHERE I went. I was low, so low I couldn't see my way up or out of this. I understood the science of HOW but I wasn't at all clear of my WHY.

As I made my way to Dr.'s appointment I met a Nurse named Ros, she was one of the first people to tell me THIS WAS GOING TO BE OK. She'd say you're not the first and you will not be the last. She gave me a reason to become excited about every visit! I'm sure she understood the road ahead of me wasn't going to be easy and therefore made a conscience decision to be a light (maybe she'd experienced my situation first hand and had compassion for me or maybe she was just God's LOVE manifested here on earth). We would only spend a couple minutes together but it seemed like she purposely used every moment to GIVE ME NEW HOPE! My Grandfather was also a huge confidence builder, he would often say to me "hold your head up, this will all be ok". He wanted me to know I wasn't alone in this walk of shame, he would say "You not the first and you won't be the last…. Pawpaw LOVES YOU". He wasn't being passive about what I had did BUT HE WANTED ME TO KNOW, THIS ISN'T THE END OF YOUR LIFE………IT'S JUST A MOMENT IN IT.

Every decision in our lives offers us a lesson bigger than ourselves. We must on purpose pay attention to what it came to teach us AND be willing to BELIEVE that this to can/will work in your favor, *IF YOU LET IT.*

For me it was being a teen mom, for you it could be something else but no matter what it is/was YOU ARE NOT WHAT YOU DID!

I'VE TAKEN ALL THE BROKEN PIECES OF MY LIFE AND SURRENDER THEM TO GOD, ALLOWING HIM TO CREATE A MASTERPEICE.

I DIDN'T KNOW IT THEN, BUT SHE WAS THE BEST THING THAT COULD HAVE EVER HAPPEN TO ME. HER VERY PRESENCE PUT A DEMAND ON ME TO BE………. BETTER!

Life moves fast, so don't forget
to acknowledge those that inspire
you.

Thank those that help you
                    and
Hug those you can't live without

Because people are the most important piece, to this puzzle we call
LIFE

~Kellie Lehner

Have you ever
had Someone
Give You HOPE?

I mean you go from
holding your head
all the way down, to
daring to lift it up
long enough to
RECOGNIZE HOPE.

I've had many encounters with people throughout my LIFE that offered me words of HOPE, but when your hearer (hearts' ear) is broken you don't know how to recognize THE GOODNESS of HOPE! BECAUSE you've become too familiar with feelings of hopelessness and your hearing becomes jaded (urban dictionary, no apology it fits ;).

I'm convinced that God sets people in specific places along your path to help repair your inner ear (heart) that the pain and shame of life altered. I have learned hurt people, hurt people BUT A HEALED PERSON CAN SPEAK HEALING TO YOUR SOUL. When your HEART is healed, you can see and hear so much clearer. When MY heart was healed, it allowed me to give HEALING away. When MY heart was healed, I could see goodness in others.

When I was hopeless those kind words gave me comfort, they started to chip away at the impossibilities I chose to believe about myself and accepted as my TRUTH. Because of those deposits I could hold my head up a little higher and stand a little taller. I still didn't know what my journey would entail BUT I knew whatever it was I wouldn't be alone in it and that I COULD DO IT!

I am A Believer that FAITH comes by HEARING and whatever you continually allow in your ear (heart) will produce.

Here's the deal YOU MUST BE WILLING, willing to accept kind words from people who mean you well. Listen to people who have your BEST interest at heart. They may not always agree with you and sometimes it may seem like what they are saying is cruel (truth doesn't always feel like LOVE, but it is). There are people assigned to YOUR Life. Pray and ask GOD to reveal them to you and while your praying ask him to remove the ones that aren't Okkkaaaaay.

Proverbs 16:24New Living Translation (NLT)
24 Kind words are like honey—
sweet to the soul and healthy for the body.

Today's struggles create tomorrows HEROS

Sometimes people won't be able to acknowledge your achievements until you die.

~Cynthia Essex

LOVE

4 Love is patient, love is kind. It does not envy, it does not boast, it is not proud. 5 It does not dishonor others, it is not self-seeking, it is not easily angered, it keeps no record of wrongs. 6 Love does not delight in evil but rejoices with the truth. 7 It always protects, always trusts, always hopes, always perseveres.

8 Love never fails. But where there are prophecies, they will cease; where there are tongues, they will be stilled; where there is knowledge, it will pass away.

1 Corinthians 13:4-8 New International Version (NIV)

HIS LOVE IS UNCONDITIONAL AND COMPLETE

Have you ever
Asked God to
Come into your Heart
And reside there?

This is the most
IMPORTANT
Page in the whole book.
In Order for everything
I have or will share
with you to WORK,
You'll NEED
HIM to STAND
THE TALLEST
Pray
Romans 10:9-11

I simply could not, have had the VICTORIES I have had, without HIM

He's waiting on YOU, to get into AGREEMENT with HIM

There was a time in my life when I had a huge hole in my soul. I over compensated in hopes that the constant tug in my soul, would be silenced by my good deeds. I tried to fill the hole with all kinds of material things. THAT DIDN'T WORK FOR ME AND IT WON'T WORK FOR YOU. Allow me to make paint a picture for you.

Do you know anyone who drink too much, stay high (using drugs of any kind), became promiscuous or is drowning in debt, trying to fill that hole? PLEASE UNDERSTAND I'M NOT JUDGING YOU AT ALL! I have done my share of hole filling and it's not cheap (emotionally or financially). Just like me, you can search the world to find something to replace the spot uniquely created for the **CREATOR** but you'll come up short every time. ANYTHING you find to place in that hole, in your soul, will be a TEMPORARY FILLER. Please believe me when I tell you, the high you get from the replacement won't last, you'll be empty again.......TRUST ME

Marvin Gaye said it BEST Ain't nothing like the real thing Baby....

If you'd like for him to come into your heart SAY THIS:

LORD JESUS I CONFESS WITH MY MOUTH AND BELIEVE IN MY HEART, THAT YOU DIED AND ROSE FOR ME. I WANT TO MAKE YOU MY LORD AND SAVIOR, IN JESUS NAME. AMEN

The search is over. He has all you need to be complete. I'm not selling you a fairy tale, genie in a bottle story. However, I am telling you, you'll have peace, direction, wisdom and a confidence that will allow you to Stand Tall in the face of Life's Adversities.

Deuteronomy 31:6The Message (MSG)

⁶ "Be strong. Take courage. Don't be intimidated. Don't give them a second thought because GOD, your God, is striding ahead of you. He's right there with you. He won't let you down; he won't leave you."

God DIDN'T choose you

BECAUSE of......

HE CHOSE YOU
in SPITE OF
HE qualifies who he CALLS

COMPLAINING

will

NEVER

CHANGE

ANYTHING

Who's your Daddy?

**Can you talk to him?
Has he validated you?
Are you REFRESHED
when you leave his
PRESENCE?**

If you prayed the prayer and asked JESUS to come into your heart, YOU HAVE A NEW DADDY, A HEAVENLY FATHER that you can tell anything. He desires the BEST for you and **HE** will never leave you ALONE!!

If you haven't had the love of an earthly father, it can be hard to grasp at first...something so AMAZING! The first question that will pop up in your head is "How can a father I don't know, LOVE me MORE than the one who biologically created me?"The TRUTH is HE'S your REAL CREATOR. The bible says he knows the very hairs on your head by number.....................A MAA ZING!!

When our earthly fathers leave a hole in our souls, we tend not to want to trust what we may consider plan B initially. Fathers who don't do their earthly part, opens the door to all types of life confusion for their children. I believe this is the ultimate plan of the enemy and the beginning of self-rejection. When you don't know, who are you, you don't know how to BE (how to be YOU, naturally or Spiritually).

One of the things we need in our lives is to be able to TRUST someone or in something. I've discovered that there is nothing I can't tell my daddy(GOD). He will listen, he will give me instructions and he won't condemn me for anything that I may say in HIS PRESENCE. Being able to stand totally naked in his presence is a process, but it is so refreshing to know when you leave his PRESENCE he won't leave you AND no matter what you just said or done, HE WILL ALWAYS LOVE YOU.

Whatever I have done that was not pleasing to him....IS DONE once I ask for forgiveness. He isn't going to bring it back up or belittle me with it. He doesn't think less of me.........HE JUST WANTS TO LOVE ME THROUGH IT and show me who I am in the midst of the situation.

Let me pause here to say whatever you do in life has NATURAL consequences and you may have to face those but he WILL be right there with you. HE WON'T LEAVE YOu.........NO MATTER WHAT!! And if you leave him, he's so LOVING he'll just patiently wait for you to call HIS NAME. HE AIN'T PETTY (urban dictionary again and again no apology…it fits), he will always respond and HE WILL ALWAYS LOVE YOU THROUGH WHATEVER!

So, if you haven't had the LOVE of yo dad…. let DADDY LOVE you
If you never had a conversation with yo dad…. Talk to DADDY
If you don't know who you are…. Let DADDY GOD show you.
If you've never had the validation from yo daddy…let DADDY validate you (he's so good at it).
If you've never had the physical touch of your dad…. let him wrap you in HIS GLORY
If your natural dad broke your heart and you have a hole in your soul

LET YOUR NEW DADDY FILL IT, YOUR HEALING IS IN HIS PRESENCE

GOD is not a situational GOD; his word says *HE WILL NEVER LEAVE YOU OR FORSAKE YOU.* We all have a hole somewhere in our souls and we all need HIM to fill it. We were created PERFECTLY ImPerFecT and he has the blueprint to build on that. Remember HE is our creator and NOBODY can take care of us like he can. He knows ALL THINGS, so EVERY answer to every question resides with/in HIM.

He supplies all that we **need** because he is a GREAT FATHER.

HE loves us so much, he created a special place on the inside of us for him to LIVE.

I LOVE THAT HE "GETS" ME. He says in HIS WORD "Before **HE** formed me in my mother's womb, he knew me". I LOVE THAT EVERYTHING about me has been PRE-APPROVED!

We didn't get to choose our earthly father but we GET TO CHOOSE TO BE IN RELATIONSHIP WITH OUR HEAVENLY FATHER and whether you choose to receive HIM or not

HIS LOVE FOR YOU IS UNCHANGING
And
LEAVING YOU IS NOT AN OPTION......EVER

If you don't have any daddy issues and you were BLESSED to have your earthly dad (or a daddy figure) present in your life, PRAISE GOD for him (I'm Praising with you)

ALLOWING DADDY GOD TO LOVE YOU,
MAKES FORGIVING YOUR BIOLOGICAL DAD POSSIBLE.

Only God can make a mess a SUCCESS

People do people things and oftentimes they don't set out to do hurt you but they do. Here is a one liner to remember

HURTING PEOPLE............. HURT PEOPLE

The next time you're faced with someone who Is mean and hateful remember, they are only giving you what they CURRENTLY have inside of them to give. They haven't made a conscience choice to just do better.

I

See

NOTHING

BUT

Opportunities

Let the YESSES
drown out the No's

You'll hear them but
**DON'T YOU DARE
ALLOW THEM TO
RULE
OVER YOUR LIFE**

We have all heard it "When Life Gives you lemons, Make Lemonade". Well I say become a lemon expert, why just make lemonade when lemons have hundreds of uses both discovered and undiscovered. By the way somebody already made lemonade.........NEXT.......... what you got?

No's should *not* discourage you, THEY SHOULD INVIGORATE YOU!! Delay doesn't mean denied. I need you to understand the path is set and the plan is Fail Proof (it will not fail). You don't know why they said *NO* and I don't know why they said *no* but what I do know is, that *no* has a PURPOSE. Smile, say Thank You and give God a praise because you are now one step closer to your YES. Don't you dare receive that NO as the end! It's just a part of the process.

A *No* just means on their level they can't help you or THEY DON'T HAVE A HEART TO HOLD YOUR VISION. MAYBE WHAT YOU WANT TO DO HASN'T BEEN DONE YET. IS IT POSSIBLE YOU ARE THE ONE WHO'LL CREATE THE BLUE PRINT FOR SOMEBODY ELSE'S YES?

If you are currently stuck in a NO situation, KEEP THE "DEFINING WHY" IN FRONT OF YOU. Defining why's will keep you driving even when you cannot see the road.

IF IT IS FOR YOU.... THERE IS A YEEESSSS

Don't put your YES in a box, IT MAY COME FROM ABOVE WHILE YOU'RE LOOKING BELOW, IT MAY COME FROM THE RIGHT WHILE YOU'RE FOCUSED ON THE LEFT. REMAIN VIGILANT YOUR YES IS NEAR.

A No only has the POWER you give it
AND FOR SOME OF US, THE NO WAS OUR YES!!

God gives you more on your way, than he does before you start!

~Dr. Ron Frierson

Keep moving.........you won't know the end in the beginning

BELIEVE

In you and all that, that entails

"How You Dreamin"
(in my Wendy Williams voice)

**Are you scaring the
Dream OR is the
Dream scaring you?**

Every GIFT you have was given to you by GOD and whether you serve him with it or not, believe in him or not, "he won't take it back". Every passionate desire you have, has an assignment attached to it to help you give birth to your DREAMS.

Sometimes we can get sidetracked with negative thinking. We'll dream BIG, BOLD and in VIBRANT colors, then we'll self-sabotage that vision immediately with a disqualifying thought. Disqualifying thoughts are dream killers, they immediately come to snatch your best life from you. Please don't believe those thoughts. YOU HAVE GREATNESS IN YOUR DNA.

I have A Dream to Inspire and Motivate Millions of People to be their BEST SELVES (yes, I'm busting me). I have a passionate desire to help people, so I do it in my own comfortable ways. Now the Dream says ok you got some street cred (somebody can vouch for me being who I say I am). Now the DREAM is calling for COMMITTMENT at another level (A BOOK, A DEGREE, A RESIGNATION). Either get on board and make it happen or put it on the shelf until later………. BUT DON'T YOU SPEAK AGAINST IT, BY SAYING WHAT YOU CAN'T DO!

LISTEN…. OPEN your mouth and combat those thoughts IMMEDIATELY with positive words like "I CAN" and "I WILL". All things are possible to HIM that can BELEVE. "I CAN WRITE A BOOK".

EVERYTHING YOU NEED IS IN YOU TO LIVE IN YOUR PURPOSES. THE NECESSARY TOOLS HAVE ALREADY BEEN PROVIDED!!! **Sometimes I wonder do we even realize how powerful we really are?**

Don't you let that Dream scare you, YOU GET UP AND CALL IT BY NAME EVERYDAY.

THE ONLY THING STANDING BETWEEN YOU AND YOUR DREAM IS YOUR STINKING THINKING

Ask God for BIG things. He created the universe. He flung the stars into space.

He Surely Can Handle Your Request

~Cynthia Essex

God Uses People to BLESS YOU

Be Careful Not to Mistreat Your BLESSINGS

Get Control of
THOSE
THOUGHTS

What YOU Be THINK'N is
What YOU BE BELIEVE'N
And What BE BELIEVE'N
Is What YOU'LL be SAY'N
Renew your mind Romans 12:2

And EVENTUALLY
THAT'S WHAT
YOU'LL BE HAVE'N

YOU spend more time with you than anyone else, SO EVERYTHING you say matters and it carries the most weight. You can talk yourself up or you can talk yourself down. It's YOUR CHOICE!

In the beginning of this book I told you about being a teen mom. It was not a good talking point from me to me BUT right before she was born I had to have a conversation with me about us. I started tuning out all the nonproductive words of others and I began speaking powerful words to myself. I KNEW I WAS GOING to be a GREAT MOM SO I SAID IT. I KNEW THAT I WOULD LOVE HER, SO I SAID IT. I knew it wouldn't be easy but I kept SAYING I COULD DO IT AND IT'LL BE OK!
BELIEVING IT WAS MOST OF THE BATTLE

When is the last time you had a positive self-talk power meeting, Lunch date or Dinner? (add a mirror so you can smile at you)

I want to challenge you to have positive words all around you, at work, at school, at home, in your car, KEEP THEM WITH YOU, NO MATTER WHERE YOU ARE! Saying these words will create BOLDNESS and build your CONFIDENCE, for your next level of LIVING. You'll see things clearer. You have the power to build you up. You don't need to wait to be affirmed by someone else. AFFIRM YOURSELF!

Next level of challenge is to hang around positive people, if they don't speak life, THEY AINT SAYING NOTHING YOU NEED TO HEAR!

There is a childhood story about "The Little Blue Engine". That little engine talked herself out of a dilemma by saying repeatedly "I THINK I CAN". And because she believed, others believed so they joined in and said "WE THINK YOU CAN" and of course the little train made it over the hill with confidence and a declaration "I THOUGHT I COULD".

SAY IT, BEFORE YOU SEE IT AND YOU'LL HAVE IT, BEFORE YOU FEEL IT

Affirmations are so important. They LITERALLY GIVE YOU LIFELINES of HOPE AND ENCOURAGEMENT. They ARE ESSENTIAL IN YOUR JOURNEY TO STANDING TALL.

You may immediately think "I don't have nor have I ever had anyone in my life to affirm me". I beg to differ, is it possible you just didn't recognize what an affirmation sounded like? We can get so comfortable with the messages of "not good enough" that we haven't an ear for affirmation. And if you don't have someone showering you with affirmations regularly. …. BLESS YOURSELF.

SOMETIMES YOU HAVE TO BE YOUR OWN LIFE COACH

When People who are in relationship with GOD need affirmation or encouragement they get to the WORD of GOD quickly. Because every great thing you need to know about you is in there. If you want to AWAKEN what you have on the inside of you, GET YOURSELF TO A WORD-BASED CHURCH AND ALLOW THEM TO MAKE YOU SO CURIOUS ABOUT THIS JESUS THANG, THAT YOU'LL HAVE TO GET IN THAT WORD AND SEE IT FOR YOURSELF!

For people who haven't discovered God for themselves yet, no worries he has placed people in your path to show you his GOODNESS. You will meet people who will make deposits into your life that make you feel **UNSTOPPABLE**. Your knower will know, that no matter what has happened to you……IT WON'T HAVE THE FINAL SAY!

He considered EVERYTHING!! If you didn't have parents, grandparents, aunts, uncles, family or friends that affirmed you, NO WORRIES. HE has every person you'll ever need ready to speak into your life. Those people will come at times and in forms you'd NEVER expect. HE will pursue you with unconditional tidal waves of LOVE and HOPE.

One **AFFIRMING WORD** can change your entire life.
Will you receive it? Will you Speak it yourself?

Life Changing Affirmations

I am the Author of my OWN LIFE STORY

I am healed Mentally, Spiritually and Physically

My mind is clothed in BRILLANCE

I am in COMPLETE control of my thought life

I am in DISCOVERY of new talents DAILY

I walk in complete forgiveness of whoever may have hurt me

I recognize that in life every lesson is a BLESSING

I replace fear with courage daily

Every Answer I need is inside of me

I am POWERFUL

Everything I put my hands to PROSPERS

Nothing can STOP ME

I am overflowing with HUMILITY

I am GRATEFUL

I am VICTORIOUS

I am predestined for GREATNESS

I am ANOINTED

I STAND up for myself.

I STAND up for what's right regardless of who's right.

I am a great TIME manager

I have Godly INFLUENCE

I am FAVORED

Grace and MERCY will follow me all the days of my LIFE

I am THANKFUL for this DAY

I am UNIQUE and I accept the things about me that make me different

I have every Godly DESIRE of my HEART

I am PERFECTLY IMPERFECT

I will live a LONG and Prosperous LIFE

My Husband LOVES me like CHRIST LOVES the CHURCH

I am a STRATEGIC THINKER

I am a CONQUER

MY PAST DOESN'T CONTROL MY FUTURE

I AM EQUIPPED TO LOVE....... AGAIN

I have FORGIVEN MYSELF

IT'S SUPPOSE TO BE HARD

(Until YOU Do It)

~Cynthia Essex

Our Limits
Only Exist in
our MINDS

For as A Man
THINKETH
In his Heart
So Is HE
Proverbs 23:7

Get out of your own way! We can't change HOW we grew up, WHO we grew up with, WHERE we grew up or things that happened when we were growing up. NOTHING about the past can be changed so let's move on (you have to decide what that process looks like for you) I'm not invalidating your childhood experiences. However, I am extending an invitation to allow those things to make you BETTER.

Some of us may have had an amazing childhood with plenty of Love, Support and few issues. Some of us may have been raised in homes with complex issues. Whatever your experience may be, choose to believe someone did the best they could to provide for you and to meet ALL YOUR BASIC NEEDS. Some of us in retrospect may now think it wasn't that bad and if it wasn't for those circumstances, YOU WOULDN'T BE WHO YOU ARE TODAY! You may think I'm nothing.... I DISAGREE, at the very least you are a SURVIVOR! And don't ever forget you are a child of the MOST HIGH GOD.....and that's WHY... you SURVIVED!

I've never met parents who looked at their baby and said "I'm going to do my best to make sure your life SUCKS". All things being equal every parent wants the very best for their children, even if they have no idea how to deliver on that desire.

If your childhood has left you with more question than answers, LET THAT GO! You CAN NOT undo what has already been done. If you cannot get clear on that, you'll be limited in how you move forward and what you can accomplish. Remember moving a little is still movement..................*Process to Progress*

I've had the privilege of meeting people from all walks of life and I've never met one without a story. Ethnically, Economically, Socially, we may be different but our human experiences are the same. Pain is pain, blood is red and hurt, hurts. No matter who you are there is only so many human experiences one can have. People who grew up without money think that if they would have had money, they would have had a different outcome. People with money wished their parents would have given them more time. People without parents think that they would have had a better shot with different parents. People with caring parents said they can be annoying and sometimes wish they'd leave them alone.

But the reality is that's just a script we made up in our heads to avoid facing the real issues of our childhood and possibly the excuse to why we aren't what we should be. You cannot change what you won't confront and if you don't choose to change it....... YOU'LL PASS THAT SAME EXPEREINCE ON TO YOUR CHILDREN AND THEY" LL PASS IT ON TO THEIRS. YOU can choose to make the BEST out of whatever your STARTER story was (everybody has one), YOU CAN DISSAPOINT EVERYONE WHO COUNTED YOU OUT or you can choose to do nothing.

CHOOSE to take ownership of your own destiny. Redefine living, color outside the lines and get out of that darn box (boxes are for things that have no life).

FOR I KNOW THE PLANS I HAVE FOR YOU DECLARES THE LORD, PLANS TO PROSPER YOU AND NOT TO HARM YOU, PLANS TO GIVE YOU A HOPE AND A FUTURE
JEREMIAH 29:11

And that is that!!! (I have a huge smile, I love this scripture)

Take every fact to the
TRUTH.

Minister Roberta Jones

Once you FORGIVE
YOURSELF
You can TRULY
begin to LOVE

(All of YOU)

I DON'T CARE WHAT YOU'VE DONE, WHATEVER IT IS, IT IS NOT YOUR DEFINER.

My life is not any different from anyone else's. I've had some GREAT days and I've had some very gray days. I've had some days I'd like to forget ever existed, but if I minus those days....... I MINUS CHUNKS OF WISDOM, LIFE CHANGING EXPERIENCES AND RELATIONSHIPS (those people you meet along the way), FUTURE MENTORING OPPORTUNTIES, AND THE ABILITY TO SHARE MY STORIES WITH OTHERS AND INVITE THEM ON THE JOURNEY OF HEALING AND SELF AWAREENESS AND FORGIVENESS.

Can you grasp it? YOU are not what happened to you. YOU are a GIFT to the earth waiting to be unwrapped! You are **not** what you did, what you did and what was done to you **happened** and you can't change that. You are not alone in whatever situation you currently find yourself in (somebody, somewhere has had or will have the same experiences and is waiting for you to help lead them to the altar of self-forgiveness).

One of reason we get stuck in unforgiveness is because we refuse to take off the t-shirt that tells everyone what we did. We think THE WHOLE WORLD (even though you haven't been outside your city limits) knows what we did, is watching and judging us (we somehow loss sight of the fact most people have their own problems and Ain't thinking about us). And the three people who really are watching and talking, is only watching and talking about you so they don't have to deal with their own mess. We think that we are the only ones that has had this experience. We keep replaying what we have done and what somebody did to use over and over (it has made the highlight reel in our minds). We've now fed that lie to our hearts.

We must not continually feed ourselves self-defeating thoughts, for doing whatever we've done. We must resist the temptation to repeatedly question HOW we could have let that happen (even if we had no control over of the situation). And even if you actively participated in it. YOU ARE **NOT** WHAT HAPPENED TO YOU! YOU ARE **NOT** WHAT YOU DID!! YOU ARE **NOT** WHAT SOMEONE DID TO YOU!

(Yes I'm Screaming....Again)

You must forgive yourself so that RESTORATIVE HEALING can begin. It's a process, but you can handle it. You must talk back to your past when it calls you. NO forwarding address, NO continuous conversations, NO sleepless nights, NO sickness or disease, NO inadequacies, NO self-defeating talk, NO regrets, NO SHRINKING....... STAND TALL AND PROFESS I AM NOT WHAT I DID. I AM NOT WHAT HAPPENED TO ME. I AM FORGIVEN AND I HAVE FORGIVEN MYSELF!

Yes, IT IS a process, you MUST denounce those thoughts one at a time. I'm not saying it'll be the easiest thing you've ever done BUT it'll BE THE BEST THING YOU'VE EVER DONE!!
I DARE YOU TO FORGIVE YOURSELF!

STOP ANSWERING TO THE WRONG NAMES
YOU ARE NOT WHAT THE PAST KEEPS CALLING YOU

YOU ARE FORGIVEN

Shake off the self-pity, shake off the defeat and get ready for God to do something new.

It Is your Turn

~Cynthia Essex

Let them FOLKS GO!
Forgiveness is a GIFT

Ephesians 4:32

[32] And be ye kind one to another, tenderhearted, FORGIVING ONE ANOTHER, even as God for Christ's sake has forgiven YOU

Act Fast This is one GIFT that will keep on GIVING

Now that you have you forgiven you…. *FORGIVE OTHERS.* Forgiveness is a dish best served warm and right from the HEART. Do it for you and WITHOUT any expectations of others. Forgiveness doesn't always look like that picture you've dreamed up in your head, it doesn't always have the Happily Ever After you've seen in the movies (**that** was written in a script, for your entertainment….).

I really struggled in this area especially with people older than me because I kept associating age with maturity. In other words, people of a certain age and or title should just know better. It took me a lot of time and a GREAT mentor (Thank You Guuurrllll) to get over it. She was willing to keep repeating the same words to me until I got it. I'm so grateful to her for her willingness to assure my future would not be held up by my inability to forgive based on a belief I had. So, if it seems like it's taking you a while to get there, YOU'RE NOT ALONE. I had to finally make up my mind to close out that chapter of my life, **FORGIVE** and **MOVE ON**.

Forgiving others will break their power over you, so the forgiver may not want to hand that power over willingly. If holding that thing over your head has gotten them "a" desired result (money, sympathy, control) they will do whatever they can, to continue the gains of manipulation. Recognize it for what it is, forgive and move on. Do you know there are people, dead and gone that are still controlling folks FROM THE GRAVE?

You'll have to determine "the how" you'll do it, only you will know what will work for you. **BE open to the opportunity and be QUICK to move on it.** For some people, it'll be a conversation you'll have to have from afar. For some people writing a letter will work out best. Sometimes counseling will be necessary. Some people will not have the opportunity to have a face to face conversation for whatever reason. YOU'LL JUST HAVE TO DO IT BY FAITH....... *JUST DO IT SO YOU TOO CAN BE FORGIVEN.*

Here is a truth. It's easier for us to forgive others than it is for us to forgive ourselves, that's why I started with you. If you can truly forgive you, YOU REALLY CAN FORGIVE ANYBODY. Forgiveness transforms and cleanses. It completely opens you up to begin trusting again. Forgiveness **DOES NOT** mean you are in agreement with what has happened to you. It just means you are ready to go into a better space. It means that you have taken back your power AND HEALING CAN NOW BELONG TO YOU. It also doesn't mean you are required to have them in your space.
It's simply a HEART RELEASE.

Operating in UNFORGIVENESS is like sticking
your head in a septic tank and
taking slow steady breathes,
it'll eventually contaminate you
from the inside out.

FORGIVENESS IS KEY

You can't soar with eagles if you are hanging out with chickens!

Send Them Cluckers Away

~Cynthia Essex

CELEBRATE YOU

You Deserve It

HIGH FIVE YO'SELF, YOU ARE A SURVIVOR! You have survived things, that made…. OTHERS QUIT. No one knows your story better than you. No one knows what it takes for you to get out of the bed but you. NO one knows what it takes for you to make it through a day, better than you. And what I'm willing to bet, is that you push thru for others and not necessarily YOU. Others are counting on us and we do not want to disappoint THEM!

We take the time to celebrate EVEYBODY else. We will give our last to someone in need. We have no problem increasing their self-worth. We make it a priority to say kind words and do nice things for others. We can always find the good in others. Why don't we take the time to invest in ourselves the same way? I'm laughing as I write this because we literally leave the mirror after complaining to anyone in the house who will listen about our butts, thighs, fat, hair, etc. AND go right into the world and COMPLIMENT, COMPLIMENT COMPLIMENT!

LADIES let's face it we are the "feel good" suppliers for everyone connected to us. And we'll give it so effortlessly to anything and anyone. But our tongues seem to tire out and our energy level isn't quite the same, when we are in need of the **same** unselfish, celebratory praise we continually give away.

We MUST get to that place, where serving ourselves the BEST STEAK on the FINEST CHINA is the norm and not the exception to the rule.

When was the last time you developed **your** skillsets? When was the last time you thought "me first"? When was the last time you invested in **your** DREAMS? When was the last time you allowed yourself to be poured into? When was the last time you said to yourself "I'm Proud of YOU"? When was the last time you said no to a "dead thing"? When was the last time you had an open and honest conversation **with** you about you? Have you made the decision to stop giving away, valuable pieces of you to undeserving people? When was the last time **YOU CHOOSE YOU**?

When I was raising my children, I would honor myself with mommy treats (yes, I created this JUST FOR ME). I would pull up to Dairy Queen with children in tow and order ONE Dairy Queen treat for me (I know some of you are freaking out and judging me) but NOBODY DIED. It was necessary to teach my children that celebrating me was ok, they had already mastered the "taking" thing, there is nothing wrong with a lesson in BALANCE.

Imma wait for you to finish, I hear you judging me, and I refuse to give you a finger, THAT WAS THE OLD ME............welllllllllll

STOP getting caught up in the day to day shuffle of taking care of everybody else. Treat yourself to something special every now and then. That something doesn't have to be a "thing", it could just be preparing for your week (not having to rush, is a gift). PLEASE take the time to speak LIFE to your LIFE (say some kind words to you and start with those **thighs**...WAIT that may just be me...carry on). Drop the kids off at school glance in the mirror and say "Let's have a Great Day Beautiful". What you about you is more important than ANYTHING ANYONE ELSE SAYS ABOUT YOU!!!

YOU BE your biggest cheerleader. YOU are in complete control of your day to day JOYS. Don't become comfortable with ignoring yourself (God gave us teenagers for that). Create a ~~RULE~~ LAW for yourself to TAKE the time to build yourself up throughout your day. It could be an ice cream, singing your favorite song, a stroll outside, or just some quite time to reflect on how far you've come and how BLESSED you are. It really doesn't matter, as long as it makes YOU FEEL CELEBRATED!!

It is ok to CELEBRATE YOU in the presence of others WITHOUT APOLOGIES and or THEIR PERMISSION.

Don't Get in
YOUR OWN WAY
Honor Yourself by TRUSTING the PROCESS

LOVE
YOURSELF
FIRST

You are the
TEACHER
of ALL THINGS,
YOU

We spend ridiculous amounts of time throughout our lives trying to be accepted by others, when self-acceptance is most important. You must Love yourself beyond every "bad" situation you've found yourself in. You've done NOTHING so bad, that it should cause you to be self-destructive. You are Perfectly Imperfect and that's what makes you Perfectly You. You are the best gift you'll ever receive, NOW THAT YOU KNOW, ACT LIKE IT.

It is NOT selfish to embrace SELF LOVE

Denying yourself Self-Love will eventually draw to you people who will validate all the reasons why YOU DON'T LOVE YOU (been there). If you don't LOVE yourself, you'll always compromise to have the approval of other people.........

WHAT YOU COMPROMISE TO KEEP, YOU LOSE ANYWAY

When you give yourself permission to LOVE you FIRST, everything else will fall into place. Having healthy Self Love will teach others how to properly love you. Offenses can't stick to you because you know who you are. You won't have to be a people pleaser for love (you can add the word NO back to your vocabulary). IF LOVING ME IS WRONG............I don't want to be right;).... JUST SO YOU KNOW

IN ORDER TO STAND TALL, YOU MUST LOVE YOU

Love yourself enough to let go of anything or anybody that makes you feel less than LOVED. People by nature are takers. You must work hard to prioritize you, because if you don't NO ONE ELSE WILL.

Here's a real warning....... PEOPLE WHO DON'T LOVE THEMSELVES, WILL NEVER BE ABLE TO FULLY LOVE YOU.

LOVE YOURSELF FOR WHO YOU ARE AND KEEP LOVING YOURSELF TO BECOME WHAT YOU ARE YET NOT.

When you allow CHANGE in your life, YOU become a LIFE CHANGER.

And that change will always be good

When you spend so much time trying to fix others, it's easy to forget that hole you needed mending.

~Shaunte Robinson

LOVE
Others
It's a
GAME CHANGER

John 3:16

There was a time when I cared nothing about people because I felt mishandled and betrayed by people, people who should have held my heart with more care. "These people" were the cause of some of my most painful memories. The reality is we've all hurt and been hurt by people. There really isn't a way to avoid "life hurt". You can't avoid it because it's kind of hard to live without people and "People will always do People Things", and although those things are not always intentional, they may still be hurtful. Sometimes you must take into consideration that, *they just didn't know any better.*

WE ARE COMMANDED TO LOVE OUR NEIGHBORS, AS WE LOVE OURSELVES the problem comes when we don't LOVE ourselves.

You are not responsible for how they treated you but you are without any doubt RESPOOONNNDDSIBLE for how YOU TREAT THEM.
Your RESPONSE IS YOUR RESPONSIBILITY.
You can shrink back, be bitter and be just like them.
OR you can **Stand Tall and TRUST IN LOVE**.

People are kind of a BIG DEAL to God so they must be more of a big deal to us. You won't be able to survive without people, you won't be able to achieve without people. GOD USES PEOPLE to accomplish his works here on earth, so you need them, there is no way around it.... *sooorryyy.*

YOUR BEST DAYS WILL BE ENJOYED WITH PEOPLE. The next time you attend a gathering listen to the memories that are shared, most people don't sit around and talk about what they did alone, they talk about what they accomplished with people. God designed HIS system to work THROUGH people, so we must be willing to *LOVE* people right where they are. When I get "people stuck" I go to GOD and ask him to show them to me the way HE SEES THEM and usually what he reveals to me gives me insight and a renewed grace for them.

This DOES NOT mean I must like (like is a choice) them or forget what they may have done to me or how they treated me, however it does mean that I recognize that I too have fallen short and mishandled people. I simply repeated what I learned and what I had learned, I had to practice over and over because our hearts weren't created to hold on to hate. I had to seek GOD and allow him to heal my heart, and it didn't happen overnight. The process is challenging but it is worth it. The weight of hate is so much heavier than the JOY of LOVE.

For God so LOVED the WORLD that he GAVE HIS ONE and ONLY SON, that whoever believes in him shall not perish but have everlasting LIFE!!!

LISTEN I don't know about you, but there is **NO ONE** currently walking this earth that I would literally surrender any of my sons LIVES for. Now **You** *might* be a little better than me so go ahead and think about it I'll wait.

HIS LOVE for us CHANGED THE ENTIRE GAME, HE LOVED US SO MUCH HE GAVE US HIS BEST GIFT AND HE GAVE FIRST.

The BEATIFUL thing is YOU DID NOTHING TO EARN IT and YOU CAN DO NOTHING TO LOSE IT.

LOVE is like climbing a mountain the higher you go the better the view. It is best utilized when you share it. We must make a choice to LOVE. We ARE Commanded to do so.

John 13:34-35 The Message (MSG)
34-35 "Let me give you a new command: Love one another. In the same way, I loved you, you love one another. This is how everyone will recognize that you are my disciples—when they see the love you have for each other."

Remember that HURTING PEOPLE......hurt people and
HEALED PEOPLE can only HEAL PEOPLE, so consider
yourself a good ole dose of healing for many.

*LOVE is the MOST POWERFUL FORCE in the UNIVERSE and
IT NEVER EVER FAILS......NEVER!*

Are You Ready
for a *little*
Vulnerability?

Trust Yourself
And Own Your
STORY!

Let me take this moment to share something with you. Before I started writing about Vulnerability I had to take the time to reassess myself. I literally closed my laptop and walked away for 3 DAYS.

I have forgiven others and I've done the tougher work to forgive myself. I have chosen to LOVE others, not because I'm so great but BECAUSE God Loves me DESPITE MY IMPERFECTIONS. Remember the commandment is to LOVE not like (but the more you Love, the harder it is to remain in dislike). At some point you just accept people where they are, accept that they are imperfect just like you and don't take offenses sooo personal and *MOVE ON*.

Sometimes You Must LEAVE people where YOU FOUND THEM!

I'm not going to lie to you, if you've ever been hurt by someone you trusted, being available to be vulnerable **again** is challenging. That doesn't mean you can't do it and yes you run the risk of being hurt again and again and again by people who are not worthy of your story or who have yet to fully own theirs. Don't you dare allow those experiences to shut you completely down because if you do, you'll never be able to experience the Beauty of witnessing your weaknesses continually transform into new strengths.

Being vulnerable will require you to continually have honest dialogue with yourself first and then with people who are assigned to you. I must repeatedly give myself permission to be vulnerable. You must talk yourself through all the tough moments. I remind myself that "this situation, isn't that situation and that person, isn't this person". Real relationships will require openness, honesty and nakedness (vulnerability). Please note that every person isn't entitled to the same level of vulnerability. You must listen to that still small voice that will direct you in how much, if anything at all to share with people at any given time. The more you trust GOD with it, the more comfortable you'll become with it and the more comfortable you become with it, THE MORE LIVES YOU GET TO WITNESS CHANGING.

THERE IS POWER IN OWNING YOUR STORY

THERE IS MORE POWER IN SHARING YOUR STORY

There are only so many human experiences one can have and once you accept that, you'll realize we are more alike than we are different. I can guarantee that whatever has happened to you has happened to someone else, no matter how crazy it may be............TO YOU.

YOU ARE NOT ALONE
TRUST GOD

Love

Your

Imperfections
You Were Created Perfectly Imperfect

~Cynthia Essex

Don't Quit

The Rewards may seem
far away BUT
They Are There

YES!! YOU have done the hard inner work and your POSTURE is looking good. Stand Tall and be proud of you. No one can *take* away what you've accomplished, but you can certainly hand it to them. Protect this new posture with all you have. Strike a BOLD STAND and hold your head up high.

Scientific studies show that a person who is willing to fail WILL EVENTUALLY HAVE SUCCESS. They become great strategist because they won't fail the same way twice. They allow life to be a classroom and they keep LEARNING. ACCEPT that it may not always go exactly as planned the first time BUT **nothing** will come to you if you quit!

The power is in how you view yourself in the situation. Do you see yourself as a failure or do you see yourself as a *revolutionary*? You are BRILLANT. YOU ARE CREATING NEW LANES AND DISCOVERING NEW THINGS. Your mistakes are about to make you rich. You have learned things that a book could never have taught you. You get to take all of your life lessons with you, on your JOURNEY to the "thing" you were in search of. Don't be surprised when that "thing" has led you to a place that takes your BREATHE AWAY.

You have grown and your work wasn't in vain but you must remain in hot pursuit of "The Best You". Those old habits may try to creep back into your Thinking but you'll have to commit to paying attention and not letting them overtake you. YOU are in complete control and you get to decide what your life looks like. Remember Your Response to life is YOUR RESPONSIBILITY!

If you write the vision and keep it before you, QUITTING WILL NOT BE AN OPTION because those big DREAMS and VISIONS are now attached to your HEART.

WHEN YOU THNK ABOUT QUITTING, REMEMBER WHY YOU STARTED!

You might not like the cards you've been dealt, but I assure you they've been shuffled. The cards in your hand can make you a winner, if you play them right.

~Jahari Essex

START YOUR DAY with a

SMILE

They're CONTAGIOUS

BE PROUD
OF
YOUR
SCARS
They Testify

Being scarred can carry elements of guilt, shame and embarrassment for years. Scars can be external as well as internal. They can be reminders of painful events in our lives OR they can become testimonies to anyone who's ever thought they'd never survive.

I remember going to the dentist one day and purposely covering my scar. I started talking to the hygienist and it took my mind off, of keeping my scar covered. As she laid the chair back she noticed the scar and stopped talking to me. She immediately reached for my file and I thought nothing of it. She started asking me very specific questions. She initiated every question with understanding and compassion. Eventually she shared with me that her brother had a scar just like mine. I remember thinking to myself in that moment "Why are you afraid of people seeing that scar"? And hiding it this time could have been expensive.

On June 9, 2013, I collapsed at church and was diagnosed with an enlarged heart. About a year later I had to have a surgery that left a scar. Every time I looked at the scar it reminded me that I failed, so I tried to cover it all the time. I was angry with myself for not having enough Faith to bypass the surgery. I was angry with God for not fixing this in the year between the collapse and the surgery. It created an insecurity in me because I thought it detracted from my superficial beauty, it was embarrassing and that it showed the world that my Faith wasn't strong enough to produce a miracle. I had allowed what happened to me to be my new definer. Once again, I was willing to rob myself of the opportunity to share my story of SURVIVAL!

THIS SCAR WAS PROOF, THAT I MADE IT THROUGH A NEAR DEATH EXPERIENCE. MY SCARS ARE BEAUTIFUL! MY JOURNEY IS MY OWN AND IT MAKES ME UNIQUE.

What happens when it's internal scarring? You probably know someone with a bad temper but they keep that thing hidden in public UNTIL someone hits the **RIGHT** button or uses the wrong tone! Owwwee that show is ticket worthy. The outburst is never about what it started out being about, it was about an internal scarring that had been hidden.

Whether it is an internal scar or external scar, we treat them all the same way. We work overtime trying to hide them. Do you know that no matter what you do to hide them, they will eventually be revealed somehow, someway? And once they are revealed you'll be asked the question "What happened to you"? Will you go for the sympathy card? Will you offer an explanation? Or will you own it and share your story of survival.

There is so much BEAUTY in your scars, no matter how you acquired them. And there I was letting my scar place limits on my life. NO MORE!

My scars represent HEALING and sharing them is an invitation to FREEDOM for others. I no longer fear them being seen, in fact it's an OPPORTUNITY for me to share my story and add perspective to what someone else may be going through. HONESTLY most of the time I don't even see it any more.

Honor your scars, the sooner you believe they have beauty, the more BEATIFUL they will become.

YOU WILL BE AMAZED BY THE PEOPLE WHO FIND HEALING IN YOUR SCARS

Stop Apologizing for WHO you are.

God Created YOU

You Are more AMAZING than any human can comprehend.

The Mirror

What do you SEE?

When is the last time you used a mirror for something other than a superficial checklist?

- ✓ Hair
- ✓ Makeup
- ✓ Outfit
- ✓ Body
- ✓ Face

We all do it; I don't know anyone who leaves home without having a quick mirror visit (welllllll…. never mind I'm not judging). I'm not implying that you should not use a mirror for these things. However, the mirror CAN be used as a Powerful tool of TRUTHS, which is why we use it to check ourselves before we go out into the WORLD. The mirror gives us the opportunity to see AND fix ourselves up, before anyone else identifies the things that need our attention. After all we are looking for what's wrong………….. aren't we?

I don't believe we use the mirror to its fullest capacity. In the mirror is where I encourage myself. In the mirror is where I found the strength to embrace my scar. In the mirror is where I learned to accept all of me. It's the place where I can be the first to SMILE at me. I often wish myself the BEST DAY EVER! It is the place that I validate me. It is also the place where I have some very HONEST conversations with myself. Remember the line from Snow White "Mirror, Mirror on the wall who's the fairest of them all"? And for many years she got the same response until the mirror was compelled to tell the new truth. Sometimes you must stand Eyeball to eyeball with the mirror and allow the truth of God's Love for you to shine through. YOU REALLY ARE PERFECT THE WAY YOU ARE. I remind myself that NO MATTER WHAT IMPERFECTIONS I FIND and MAGNIFY IN THE MIRROR, or what Powerless words I may utter to myself, about myself……..**GOD LOVES ME!**

In the morning, I reflect on my yesterday and I take the time to get clarity on my what and my why's (what I did and why I did it). After I take a self-inventory and have a TRUTHFUL conversation with me, I take the time to speak into myself. I build myself up, I validate my worth and I don't become consumed with the small Imperfections I may see.

What's funny is the mirror has no bias, it only sees what you see! If you see beauty, it sees beauty. If you see an amazing being, it sees an amazing being. If you see healing, it sees you healed. If you see hope, it sees hope. If you see a BLESSING, IT SEES A BLESSING.

LOVE YOUR REFLECTION AND WATCH IT EVOLVE
You will NEVER see, what you NOT looking for

"Take a moment each day to incorporate a hint of sparkle, you never know when that glisten may catch your eye to new innovations that will light the way to your next adventure."

-Lisa Willard

Are You Ready to
BE

STRETCHED?

JESUS......

I remember worshipping GOD and telling him I was ready to sell out to him and I WANTED CHANGE IN MY LIFE. I WANTED TO BE JUST LIKE HIM! I sewed into it, I confessed it. I was ready......SO I THOUGHT.

Soooooo let's talk about this! IT DID NOT COME EASY. I would have liked for him to wave a magic wand or sit on the front porch with me and coach me on the 5-point system to change and if not that, at simple MEMO that need only say Guurrrllllll put on your seatbelt.

When these opportunities of change showed up, they didn't resemble what I asked GOD for (they NEVER do and they NEVER will). In fact, they didn't resemble any good thing that would come from a Good God. I endured one affliction after another. Parts of it even seemed inhumane. I began to think I did something wrong. I kept trying to figure out where I MISSED IT because this wasn't what I PRAYED for. However being stretched feels like you've missed it. It feels like you are being punished. Sometimes it feels like God has abandoned you. I wish I could tell you I UNDERSTOOD what has happening, but I didn't and since I didn't understand it I TOOK IT ON MYSELF, I tried to handle it....MY WAY (and that didn't turn out well AT ALL). I searched all parts of me trying to get *right* so these growing pains would end.

We either allow the stretch or we break.

And while I was busy trying to survive my heart was changing. I was being stretched and I did not recognize the presentation of this GIFT because God forgot to wrap it in pretty paper. You may be asking yourself, WHY I would call it a gift after hearing words associated with pain. I call it a gift because I finally allowed myself to give into the stretch. I had to trust GOD in what seemed like a slow death.

I was in the midst of an unfavorable situation and I reminded God of a WORD he had given me, as I was facing a discipline slip that was conjured up as weapon of revenge. I think I would have been OK if it was true, but the truth of the matter was it was only a weapon, manifested in form of a discipline slip (but it had no prospering power). As I stood there I said God you said, "No Weapon Formed against me would Prosper-(Isaiah 54:17)" HE REPLIED "IT WON'T". It was so sweet and calm (it really made me mad at the time) because I had the weapon in my hand. It was tangible and it was written. The problem was I didn't have a revelation of the scripture, it never said the weapon would not form, it said it would not prosper. The truth is, **if** it never formed HOW would I KNOW, it didn't have prospering power? If I was never sick, HOW would I KNOW he was a healer? If I was never broke, HOW would I KNOW he was a provider? If I was never Lost, HOW would I know, I WAS SO IMPORTANT TO HIM THAT HE WOULD COME AND FIND ME?

The promise will require a stretch, that stretch is required to see the PROMISE manifested!

I share with people every chance I get that, that was THE BEST THING that ever happened to me. I just couldn't see it at the time. These stretches made me more compassionate, it helped me hear GOD clearer, it gave me my voice back. It made me fear less and trust him more. It created boldness. It showed me multiple things about myself, because the stretch WASN'T ABOUT THE TOOL BEING USED TO STRETCH ME, IT WAS ABOUT ME. IT WAS ABOUT MY FUTURE. IT WAS ABOUT YOU. IT WAS A PART OF MY JOURNEY. IT HAD ALREADY BEEN COUNTED IN IT.

WHAT HE HAS FOR YOU IS FOR YOU! YOU JUST HAVE TO STAND TALL enough to receive it. AND YOUR STRENGTH IS IN YOUR STRETCH.

I'm A LIVING WITNESS

The very next big stretching opportunity I had in my life, I remembered this lesson and I began speaking the WORD over my life a little faster ;)

The scripture says:

[71] *It was good for me to be afflicted so that I might learn your decrees.* Psalm 119:71

Stop Counting Your problems
when
LIFE HAS SO MANY
POSSIBILITIES

~Cynthia Essex

I'm the ONLY
one who can STOP
ME!

When you Get THIS......NOTHING ELSE WILL MATTER

Sometimes
It's HARD to
imagine what
you can't
SEE

However, You CAN be, what you didn't see.

An **AUTHOR**?!! Who **ME**?!! Who would have thought, better yet who would have had the nerve to think the thought that I could/would become an Author? I know that people write books, they do exist……………… BUT ME?!

I didn't grow up around people doing extraordinary things. Don't misunderstand me, I was surrounded by hard working "normal" people. I don't remember anyone writing books or many business owners. When I was young, working in the plant was the BIG to-do. A job that paid well, had good benefits and was very predictable. Do the time, and RETIRE with a reasonable pension and that was that.

I was fortunate enough to grow up with a mother who exposed us to everything she could. Not only did she expose us, she also invested in other children by taking them with us. I believe some of those kids would not have been introduced to "More" without her.

As parents of 8 children it was a high priority to introduce our children to anything outside of the 4 walls of our city and state. We didn't want them to be afraid to travel. Five of our eight children currently live outside of Michigan and two of the remaining three plan to call another state home. And although we exposed them to new places, we couldn't afford to take them everywhere but the seed was planted and now they have gone further than us.

I MISS THEM SO MUCH, BUT I LOVE THAT THEY WEREN'T AFRAID TO GO.

All of our children have been exposed to **entrepreneurship.** My husband is a Drywall Finisher and he has been self-employed most of their lives. He is the kind of person that isn't afraid to try anything. He has attempted many things; some have failed and some have been successful. However, what I LOVE about him, is the failures NEVER stopped him from trying something else NEW.

It's hard to imagine what you can't see. Exposure is everything and if no one took the time to help you see it, take ownership of your life and start imaging and if you're already imaging, IMAGINE BIGGER. Exposure will give your mind something to run away with and it'll give your HEART a HOPE ANCHOR.

I believe that this is a $\textbf{HUGE}$ key to creating a LIFE CANVAS for yourself and subsequently your children and their children.

You may not be able to see it in your current life, BUT what is stopping YOU from seeing it in a book, on TV or in living color on the internet. You are limitless in what you can paint on the tapestry of your heart and once your heart grabs it, YOU WON'T BE ABLE TO SHAKE IT OFF. HaHa you can't UNSEEN IT!!

IMAGINATION makes it possible to experience a whole world inside YOUR mind.

What you are asking for isn't impossible

impossible

You're just asking the wrong people.

They have limited vision

~Cynthia Essex

UNLOCK
Your
Own Cell

You have the Key

YOU are not a prisoner because you've always had the keys, SO stop acting like one.

I know that the cell locked when they closed the door:

-Who rebounds from what you've had happen to you? They threw everything at you and it didn't kill you, in fact it made you stronger BUT you couldn't see your own strength because you've always had to fight. SO, FIGHT…. but not for everyone else, fight for you! I know you see the locked door as isolation but remember doors keep people in and they also keep people out. You may not have chosen this cell but this locked door has just given you more FREEDOM than you currently realized.

I know you heard the finality of that door slam;

-They told you, you weren't going to be nothing because your momma ain't nothing and your daddy ain't nothing. You see the same thing they see, you've done the math 1 nothing + 1 nothing = 3 nothings! Even you have counted you out. I'm asking you to count it again *"they"* seen this all wrong *"they"* hadn't considered that 1 Life plus another Life created **LIFE**! That **LIFE** has an opportunity to be ANYTHING including **FREE**……

I know you see the bars separating you from them;

The only barrier keeping you in the cell is in your mind. Get up and move your feet. Stop thinking *they* are better than you, that they have an advantage because *they* do not. You have the same 24hrs, you have the same abilities and your secret to successes is being held captive by your inability to see beyond those bars. *Get Out Your Own WAY*

I know you see them walking around with the keys;

YES, they have it all and if you just had, what they have YOU would surely be living a happier more fulfilled life…RIGHT?…WRONG!!

Those keys they have aren't for you. The keys they have are specifically for them, they are not yours. EVERYTHING you need to BECOME a keyholder has already been provided. Every key to unlock every success is on the inside of you. You see what works for one individual, will not necessary work for another. You can share principles but you'll need to seek inward for application.

Don't be so busy looking at their keys that you lose sight of this fact; them possessing keys means that…… they too had a cell.

YOU ARE AS FREE AS YOU THINK
You have ALWAYS had the KEYS!

Make choices that empower
you,
not that imprison you

~Loyce Seals Brown

ASK!

You have NOTHING TO LOSE

Why are we afraid to ask for what we want?

Often, we don't ask because we don't want to hear NO......Hey I get it; it's not like you've ever heard it before.

-Or are we afraid of the yes because we aren't ready for the responsibility that comes with it.

-Maybe it's because, we don't KNOW what we want.

-It is possible we are afraid they will laugh at us

-We don't believe we are WORTHY of a yes......

-We anticipate failure

-We allow ourselves to be talked out of BETTER

-We don't want to lose our friends

-We don't really believe in our DREAM

Eliminate Excuses and STOP waiting for what you want to come to you, GO GET IT.

IF YOU DO NOT ASK, YOU WILL NEVER KNOW IF YOU COULD HAVE HAD IT AND FEAR WILL HAVE DONE ITS JOB

DISCOVER

Who you are? And Why you are here?

DEVELOP

Once you discover who you are and why you are here, WORK hard to build your skillset in those areas (*yes you have many purposes*). God gave you those specifically to be a BLESSING to others and if you don't get in position the world will miss out. Face this fact that *you will never be able to ignore the gifts inside you.*

DEMONSTRATE

BAKE the cake, ENCOURAGE people, OPEN the business, BUILD the house, COACH the kids, TEACH the women, GROW people's money, BE a Mother, DEVELOP strategies, SING the songs, WRITE THE BOOK! (YES, I'm Yelling Again)

Discover, Develop and Demonstrate ~ World Overcomers Church International

Once you KNOW it...It is your responsibility to GROW it.
Give to IT and IT will give to you.

TODAY IS YOUR DAY

Do what you said you'd do tomorrow

It's MORNING

WAKE Uuuup

I LOVE WAKING UP IN THE MORNING!! I ALWAYS HAVE A SMILE ON MY FACE AND THE FIRST THING I SAY IS Good Morning to my **DADDY** and then I say **THANK YOU!** I **I** Don't take mornings for GRANTED, SOMEBODY DIDN'T HAVE ONE

My grandmother would say "I'm thankful for being in the land of the Living, and clothed in my right mind." As a child, I had no idea what this meant. But as an adult who has seen all kinds of troubles.........I GET IT. The ability to think clearly is such a BLESSING and by clearly, I don't mean you get up and you have no problems. But you have the ability to recognize and resolve them on your own. You can simply face the day with your whole mind engaged. Have you ever had life burden you to the point, where your thinking was impaired?

What I love about the morning is darkness cannot stop it from coming. No matter what the night brought…. MORNING IS STILL RUNNING ON SCHEDULE, IT WON'T BE DELAYED, IT'LL ALWAYS BE ON TIME…IT IS CONSISTENT!

I can honestly tell you I have gone to sleep exhausted from life happening and WAKE UP so refreshed, renewed and filled with HOPE.

Me waking up is a reminder that God still has work for me to do. It is yet another day to do and share what I Love. It is a day that will be filled with Love, Laughter, Life and Life Lessons. It is a day I'll never see again.

Sometimes mornings do not include a visible Sun but that doesn't negate the fact that it's still morning and the Sun is still in position. BECAUSE MORNING KNOWS IT 'S PURPOSE!

You will NEVER see,
what you are
NOT looking for

~Cynthia Essex

Can you list 10 things you are grateful for?

If you consciously give thanks for them daily, watch the list grow and your life change!

Good Night

If you SLEEP better,
you can
LIVE BIGGER

Previously I mentioned how I LOVE THE MORNING, but that night life is what makes my mornings so incredible.

There was a time when I didn't sleep well at all. I didn't know how to let go and just fall asleep or my sleep would be constantly interrupted. This went on for years and eventually it took its toll on my body. A lack of rest can be a contributor to poor health. My attitude was less than welcoming (I just wanted to slap everybody that said something stupid) .... is it just me that have those days? I do not care **what** you say, I'M NOT THE ONLY ONE!

I had to learn to turn off my day. I had to let go of people and the things they may have said or did, that I allowed to contribute to my day in a negative way. And one of the ways you can let them go is by making yourself a priority. If you have a bad day at work, give yourself the ride home to decompress and make it a rule that when you turn on your street, you turn off work. You must realize you are the only you, you have, and If you lose you, you can't give anything to anyone. You can take it from me or you can be like me. I had to learn the hard way the cost of not giving my body what it needed to reset. If you don't make rest a priority, YOUR BODY WLL.

We need our minds to relax. Do you know that your mind rids itself of unimportant information, while you sleep? (thank GOD)
Did you know that your body repairs itself, while you sleep?

Now when I fall asleep I REST. Whatever has happened during the day happened. I also try to fall asleep watching something funny or listening to a great life message. I believe our Spirit never sleeps, so why not feed it phenomenal super foods and position yourself for a great night of rest.

When Life isn't going right, TAKE A NAP

You'll live longer

REST

Yes, sleep is essential and so is REST. I believe that if we could learn to rest we would sleep better. Rest in knowing you are important. Rest in knowing you brighten someone's day. Rest in knowing you did your best. Rest in knowing you made the best decision you could, with what you had. Rest in knowing, that situation was out of your control. Rest in knowing you are needed. Rest in knowing you are a GREAT MOM. Rest in knowing another opportunity is coming. Rest in being who God has called you to be. REST. Rest in knowing you are prepared for this life. Rest in knowing you can move on without them. Rest in knowing everybody gets hurt. Rest in knowing you are never alone. Rest in knowing trouble don't last always. Rest in knowing you are not a mistake. Rest in knowing your latter days will be greater than your past. Rest in knowing you are enough. REST. Rest in knowing the hard tests are a part of your testimony. Rest in knowing you don't have all the answers. Rest in knowing someone is always praying for you. Rest in knowing you may have to walk alone but you can. Rest in knowing you are more than a conquer. Rest in knowing you are not what someone called you. Rest in knowing everyone won't know your worth. Rest in knowing as you grow, some will go. Rest in knowing everything you need is inside you. Rest in knowing vengeance belongs to God. Rest in knowing the battle is not yours, it's the Lords. Rest in knowing you are good enough. Rest in knowing YOU WERE WORTH DYING FOR. PLEASE REST.

Just fall back into HIS ARMS and REST

(it is a process, perfected with practice)

Why Me

why not..................you are a problem solver

List 5 Things that you want to
ACCOMPLISH in the NEXT
YEAR?

YOU
are the
SOLUTION

Stop Hiding

If you can train your brain to be solution minded, not only would you live a more productive life.........you'll be forever employable and YOU'LL BE FREAKIN RICH!!!

How do you approach life, are you a whiner? Or are you a closet team leader? Cynthia what is a closet team leader? I'm so glad you asked ;) A closet team leader pretends to be a whiner so they fit in with the rest of the whiners. You have idea's and solutions but you let what "they" think stop you from talking. I have something to say....................ARE you LISTENING?

YOU DON'T NEED ANYONE'S PERMISSION TO LEAD. LEADERSHIP IS DEFINED BY AN ATTITUDE...not a title.

I won't apologize for yelling............nope

From now on every single time you have a problem
THINK SOLUTION.

When you go to your boss, present the problem and then your solution. When you're in meetings and brainstorming is necessary.......... THINK SOLUTION! Please hear me, EVERYONE is not going to like it, some will think your sucking up or call you a know it all.............................but who cares because

YOU ARE GOING TO BE FREAKIN RICH!

Yes, I yelled again but you don't care because you are on your way to the
BANK.

Steve Jobs convinced people he had a solution to a problem they didn't even know they had and he is

FREAKIN RICH$$

And 5yrs from now the whiners will be in the same spot whining.

TRUST ME
They see your
Greatness

And that's the problem
.... not you

Have you ever gone back and read a high school yearbook? The comments that are written about some of classmates are unbelievable sometimes. How is it, that they could have been so right on the money with what they said?

It's funny how your greatness shines thru and you are the only one who does not see it. It's amazing how gifts and talents never sit quietly. They have a way of being noticed. Let's face it, you have something special and THERE IS GREATNESS IN YOU!

When I think about my children, I think about the individual greatness I seen in each one of them. I always made sure they knew what their strengths were. They could always trust me with their dreams because I would do whatever I could to make them come alive.

Greatness isn't always welcomed and it can be intimidating to people who have not yet found their greatness. But don't allow this to make you question your GREATNESS. Sometimes it will come from people who have more than you……. more money, more education, more connections and more support. There dismissal of you, can be confusing to you, when your only intention was to be a student in their presence. Don't be confused THEY SEE YOUR GREATNESS TOO.

Insecure PEOPLE see jealousy, when you WERE REALLY GLEENING

Surround yourself with PEOPLE who believe in YOU. Their very presence should cause you to think higher and dream bigger. YOU should swell with possibilities. You should feel HUGE and UNSTOPPABLE. Your grasshopper vision of yourself………should fade away, as you begin to transform into the DOMINATOR, YOU were CREATED TO BE!

People who cannot recognize STRENGTH in their own ability, do not possess the COURAGE to SEE YOURS

Once you KNOW
WHO you are
you
CAN'T UNKNOW it

You Were Created ON PURPOSE, FOR A PURPOSE AND THEY WON'T STOP
CALLING YOU

~Cynthia Essex

Say This:

WHAT GOD HAS FOR ME

IS FOR ME

I'm NEVER in FEAR OF NOT HAVING ENOUGH

Be Content

In Whatever State, you are In
Today

Con-tent
In a state, of
peaceful happiness
~adjective

Listen, people work overtime trying to keep up with the JONES. We spend too much time measuring our **real** lives against someone else's fake timeline. If they GOT it yesterday, we want it by the end of the week (no matter how long it took them to works it out). We have no patience with PROCESS. We want what we want and we want it NOW. We haven't quite figured out that we don't live our lives in microwaves.

Receiving anything prematurely is not ideal. Just think about the process of having a baby. We can't make a baby today, carry it 9 weeks and give birth to a healthy, happy baby. All things being equal, you want that baby to stay put for forty weeks, nothing more, nothing less. Every step of the process has a specific responsibility to this developing new life.

This truth is applicable in every area of your life. You want everything that belongs to you in its right timing. You don't want a premature marriage because all your friends are getting married. You don't want to rush being a parent because you want someone to LOVE you. Don't be in a hurry for anything. Be content where you are, WAIT and develop patience until it is your time to receive what truly belongs to you.

Today, the average household with credit card debt has balances totaling *$16,748. This debt is largely because we are not content. We must have what we want NOW. I believe we fill ourselves with stuff to satisfy our pain and to numb the resounding voice of "you're not enough" THIS IS WHAT ADDS TO OUR DISCONTENTMENT, because it's never enough and it satisfies NOTHING! AND WE HAVEN'T YET FIGURED OUT "**THINGS**" DON'T HAVE HEALING PROPERTIES.

How about looking at what's going on in your life, the next time life presents you with the opportunity to become discontent.

Try being Thankful and Grateful for everything you have right now. Somewhere, somebody is praying to God for what you are currently not satisfied with. Ask God to show you people with less. Whenever I complain I'll always meet someone who has it worse off than myself.

Try meeting a mother who can't have children, while someone else is complaining about hers getting on her nerves.

Try meeting a woman with no hair living with cancer, while you complain about a bad hair day.

Stop complaining that you have nothing at home to eat when there is homeless people eating out of trash cans.

Try meeting a man with no feet, while you complain about not having the right shoes.

If you allow a perspective shift, you WILL BE CONTENT, YOU WILL BE HUMBLED, YOU WILL BE GRATEFUL AND YOU'LL HAVE A PERFECT HEART FOR SERVE.

In Philippians 4:11, Paul said, "I have learned in whatsoever state I am in therewith to be content". The Amplified Bible describes being content as "satisfied to the point where you are not disturbed or disquieted". It doesn't say satisfied to the point where you don't want change, but satisfied for now until the change comes.

* http://www.mediatorlawgroup.com/

Shortcuts lead to
LONG ROADS

And Disappointment

Ohhh
ThOse
Storms

You make me better

I remember asking God to help me be more like him. I song, songs of surrender, I confessed the word over my life every day. I was in the zone, I wanted change so bad and I was willing to do whatever it took……

What I didn't consider and what nobody told me, is WHAT I'M GETTING READY TO SHARE WITH YOU;

If you sit down and think about it, nothing changes without a little turbulence. We can't go from one season to another season without the **WIND**. When the wind starts to blow, your location is key. Some locations are prone to violent storms. Some places transition with mild storms and others will only get wind effects. But what is clear is nobody escapes the process (wind) of *a CHANGE*.

During my quest to be more like my Jesus……IT SEEMED AS IF MY WHOLE LIFE WAS FALLING APART! Every problem brought a headache with it and eventually my unrelenting headaches turned into heartache (literally). The stress of not understanding my storms almost killed me.

I lost what I considered to be a PERFECT JOB for me in that season. I had parenting troubles, marriage troubles, work troubles……. the dog chased the cat, the cat ate the bird, the bird's momma was mad and wanted to retaliate (I had to remind her vengeance is the LORDS and that wasn't even my cat……ok). I mean it was crazy. It seemed like I was stuck in this position for years with small breaks every now and then.

I remember looking up and asking... "God HOW does all of this happen, while I'm minding my own business and pursing A GREATER GOOD"? I had wronged no one, in fact my walk was better at this point in my life than ever before. I tried to find God's hand in all of this, only to come to a temporary conclusion HE MUST HAVE ABANDONED ME (this was my pain speaking). I believed All was well with me until....... I ACTIVATED THE STORM OF CHANGE. I didn't realize what I prayed for was unfolding in my storms.

I must admit I am a storm watcher (from the convenience of my home, don't even think I'm going to find trouble), it always serves as a reminder to me that WE MUST ENDURE THE PAINS OF CHANGE, If WE WANT TRUE CHANGE in our lives.

TODAY I have no problem telling you "it was good that I was afflicted". I'm not telling you, I understood "the why's" of everything that happened to me but I COULD NOT BE THE PERSON I AM TODAY WITHOUT ALL THAT WIND, RAIN AND TUBERLANCE!

Please don't be afraid of the storm. It isn't a storm, BIGGER than the GOD we serve. AND THE RAINBOW IS A REMINDER OF HIS PROMISE TO NEVER LEAVE US ALONE.

Listen, the pains in the storms of change are much easier than the pain of staying the same.
If you remain the same, you will witness people doing things that you know YOU were called to do.
Now THAT my SISTER is painful

Faith

Won't always make sense

Trust it Anyway

Check Yo'Self

OWN your own
TRUTH

Are you, what you're asking others to be? Are you LIVING what you want to see show up in your life?

Some people live their lives with that finger in point position. They accept responsibility for nothing! It's always someone else's fault. How is it that YOU NEVER DO ANYTHING WRONG? And NOTHING IS YOUR FAULT? Are YOU the common denominator or nah?

Check Yourself

Maybe the words they spoke about you had some truth in them.

Maybe your attitude is bad

Maybe you're not integral

Maybe you're not friendly

Maybe you have a problem being loyal

Maybe you do lie

Maybe you are negative

Maybe you alienated yourself

Maybe you have a problem apologizing

YOU KNOW whether the things people say to you about you are TRUE, and shifting responsibility from you to them doesn't validate the behavior.

"Because you did this.............. I did that"

Remember we live a seeded life (some call it Karma). What you put out there will show up in your life eventually. So, I'm just saying before EVERYBODY else is wrong ALL THE TIME. Maybe you just need to Check Yo'self.

SELF CHECKS are necessary. Wouldn't you like the opportunity to address self-defeating actions before they grow out of control? People will begin to dodge you in hopes of avoiding you and your mess.

I get it, it's easier to point, assign blame and carry on, than to *OWN IT*. But have you ever considered what you are teaching the children/young people in your life? Foolish people breed foolish children. If you steal, they'll steal and WHEN they get caught, they'll surely offer you up as their defining WHY, when asked.

"When you point one finger, three are pointing back at you"
(Things Older people said)

You can't STAND TALL and make excuses at the same time.

You should make the commitment to yourself to embrace correction, whether it be by self-examination, REVELATION from the HOLY SPIRIT or by someone who LOVES you enough to tell you the TRUTH.

People who ain't going nowhere, CELEBRATE your ignorance and if you don't believe me, **CHANGE** (check yourself) and watch how fast they start talking about you *acting funny.*

Change is hard at first, Messy in the Middle and Gorgeous in the End.

~Robin Sharme

I was the common denominator in ALL my failed relationships. When I stopped making excuses and pointing the finger, I was able to shift my thinking and my behaviour!! Hold yourself to a higher standard and REQUIRE MORE FROM THOSE IN YOUR CIRCLE!

~Albany Summers

Don't Allow your scars to CHANGE your CORE

Life can make you switch it up

LIFE it happens and it can leave us bruised, banged up and sometimes just short of our perception of what dying feels like.

Earlier I talked about scars and how you shouldn't be ashamed of them because they tell amazing stories and they symbolize healing.

Let's talk about what the trauma behind the scars can do to you. It doesn't matter HOW you got the scars, whether it was your 1st love, an absent parent, a broken promise, or your first *NO* after you were confident you'd hear a yes. Or it may have been a physical hurt, someone may have been abusive to you. Here's a FACT pain is pain and hurt is hurt no matter how it came to be.

The process to dealing with pain is comparable to the five **stages of grief**. Denial, anger, bargaining, depression and acceptance.

We all move through these stages at our own pace and each stage has the power to affect our core. Our first instinct is to protect ourselves from ever experiencing that pain again (but the reality is there is NO iron clad way to protect yourself from hurt and pain).

I want to encourage you to move through the pain and after you move through it revisit every wall you may have built to protect your HEART on your way through it and begin tearing them down.

-WHEN WE BUILD WALLS, PEOPLE CAN'T SEE US FOR WHO WE ARE.

I know you said you would never LOVE again, but you must if you are a loving person in your core.

I know you said you would never GIVE again, but you must if you are a giver in your core.
I know they broke your TRUST and you said I'll never trust people again, but you must if that's who you are in your core. Trusting people give chances to people other people over look.

I know they have mistaken your big HEART for an opportunity to use you. Don't you stop loving, KEEP your heart on display and keep it open for business, because if you don't someone will miss out on the best part of GOD here on EARTH.

People do people things and sometimes those things can be detrimental to our cores. BUT let me encourage you to REMAIN SOLID IN YOUR CORE because ONCE THEY CHANGE YOUR CORE..................THEY HAVE CHANGED YOU! ONCE YOU ALLOW **YOU** TO BE CHANGED, YOU FORFEIT LIVING YOUR BEST LIFE.

I often burn my hands removing my cakes from the oven (mostly not paying enough attention to what I'm doing) BUT THAT WON'T EVER STOP ME FROM BAKING CAKES because baking is in my CORE.

You may have to do it differently and that's OK BUT PLEASE DON'T STOP DOING IT ALL TOGHETHER! Remain TRUE to your CORE.

PEOPLE
didn't
DIE
for you
JESUS DID

Remember That!

Tell the Truth

Lying is EXPENSIVE

It sounds simple BUT Lying is a real problem. It all seems harmless until you make it your way of life. I know we've made that whole "little white lie" thing socially acceptable.

I don't believe people think before they speak. And for some people I think awkward silence is an invitation to opening thy mouth and SAY SOMETHING trigger. So, we do, we open our mouths and we lie. Usually it's the ones that are thoughtless, innocent and very are complimentary.

If what you are say isn't TRUE stoooooopppppp. It just sounds mindless and insincere. Remember what comes from the heart reaches the heart and a BIG SINCERE SMILE WILL ALWAYS SUFFICE. (I know, you don't know anybody like this.........I wrote this for your neighbor).

You know you don't like her outfit, so why'd you say you did?
You know you didn't like what they said or did, so why'd you say you did? **OR** WHY DID YOU SIMPLY AGREE WITH SILENCE? (sometimes confrontation will clear up assumptions and create a dialogue for clarity)

Have you ever taken the time to listen to your own conversations? Not only listen but evaluate it at the same time?

Part of my journey in Learning to STAND TALL was to call myself out all the time AND CORRECT THE LIE. It was soooo awkward at first but It didn't take long to stop myself from lying. The very next step was to challenge myself to evaluate "The Why".

Who was I trying to impress? What was I trying to avoid? Why do I need to be whoever this lie is creating? Why don't I care enough about you, to tell you the truth? Did I need something from you? Was I hiding from me?

Look I'm not getting ready to lecture you on lying. NOPE! I just want you to consider this, when you LIE you LIE to someone and eventually they'll figure out you are a liar (even if the lie is white). At some point, CREDIBILITY, will be an issue and everything you say will be suspect. At some point the word will spread and then your new name will be LIAR. Soon you'll discover that LIAR's lie and they will eventually LIE ON YOU!
I know you always tell the truth and you don't lie, so this is for the other people.

THE BEAUTIFUL PART OF JOURNEY WAS THE SELF EXPLORATION THAT CAME WITH IT
TRUE GROWTH

Side Note: *If you must make a choice between lying and silence... ... ...choose SILENCE sometimes that within itself reveals TRUTH*

Make Sure your WORDS are SWEET

You may have to eat them.

What's the REAL Issue?

Sis
Please Press IN

There is a bible story that I love, it talks about a woman who had an issue of blood for 12 long years. She spent all she had to be cured and nothing worked. She heard about Jesus and decided he was her next HOPE.

Here she is so close to being CURED, the only thing standing between her and healing is this *crowd*.............

IF ONLY SHE COULD TOUCH THE HEM OF HIS GARMENT, SHE WOULD BE MADE WHOLE.

I want to ask you some questions. What's in your crowd? What are the things that's standing between you and JESUS or you and a dream or you and happiness?

A lot of time it is people and their shenanigans. We get our eyes and our ears fixed on them (what they think about us) and that paralyzes us. Sometimes it's all the outside distractions....TV, nonproductive Phone Calls, Social Media, being knee deep in someone else's business. Sometimes the crowd is inside you, you spend too much of your time cooperating in self-defeating behaviors, self-defeating talk and self-doubt.

I'm sure this woman had experienced everything I listed above, YET SHE PRESSED IN. She didn't allow her *unclean* state to stop her from getting what she ~~wanted~~ needed.

She found healing at the lowest part of his garment and at her lowest point in her LIFE, *BECAUSE* she made a DECISION to PRESS IN.

Not everything that is faced can be changed. But nothing can be changed until it's faced.   -James Baldwin

In order to please
God
You may have
to disappoint
a few people

EVERYBODY can't go with you

Seatbelt Needed
TURBULENCE EXPECTED

GROWTH WILL BE REQUIRED

New Level………………. New You

I assure you GOD didn't bring you this far,
TO LEAVE YOU

Count the
COST

GET PREPARED
Then Get to Work
It's Personal

Just the thought of the initial cost of something BIG can be stressful, it can literally cause you to quit (thoughts of failure begin to bombard your mind) before you've even physically begun. In the last couple of days, I have had this conversation several times. So, let's talk about it.

Everything has a cost and its initial investment may seem to be extremely high. If you're starting a business, it's the finances (office equipment, furniture, computer, pots, pans, etc..). You may have to invest your time doing research. You never escape the Paperwork for Licensing, Permits, Payroll, etc.). Ohh God let this not require a DEGREE! Now you'll have to commit to studying, homework, refocusing and becoming comfortable with DELAYED GRATIFICATION (basically sacrificing life as you currently know it, for a GREAT REWARD LATER). NOW LISTEN, the payoffs are AWESOME and worth the initial investment.

We often count the cost for "THINGS" but……….

What about the more inner-personal stuff liiiikkkkkeeee (THE YOU) in your RELATIONSHIPS!!! Remember we can't control anyone else, sooooo we must do our individual parts.

The initial cost feels like DEATH. The questions you ask God may go a little something like this.

1. You want me to KEEP LOVING who?...........Why?

2. You want me to FORGIVE who?..........Do you even know what they did?

3. You want me to GIVE them what?   Can you please find somebody else to do it?

4. You want me to GO where?......God listen I'm not trying to go near those people? I don't want to catch a case……

Side Note: Every one of those directives have a blessing right on the other side of the obedience.

The initial cost of this type of vulnerability feels like DEATH because IT IS!! IT IS DEATH TO SELF... (JESUS take the whole wheel!). The bible says we should count the cost BEFORE we build (I'm adding complain or quit). If you are serious about BUILDING, you must sit down, count the cost and consider the DIVIDENDS. I PROMISE, IF YOU RELEASE YOU (die to self) you'll find yourself LETTING GO of generational dead weight. I know it seems hard but it will become easier (easier in the sense of becoming more focused on the bigger vision, so the small things that tripped you up before, won't be an issue) and the benefits will far exceed what you could have ever imagined.

I'm going to let you in on a little secret. When God is nudging you towards GROWTH, he'll begin to bring PEOPLE into your life that will challenge you. They will share with you their testimonies about going to school, starting a Business or reconciling relationships (or at least making peace with people). YOU NEED ONLY TO BE WILLING! AND THEN OBEDIENT (yaasss action is required)!! *There is only one question I have for you.*

HOW BAD DO YOU WANT IT?

HE TRULY WILL NEVER LEAVE YOU and HE HAS THOSE LITTLE GEMS hidden for you in the JOURNEY, that will keep you moving towards the DREAM. God is on your side and HE'S SO IN LOVE WITH YOU!

WHO is worth you giving up THE BLESSING?

WHAT is worth you giving up THE BLESSING?

WHY would you want to give up THE BLESSING?

WHEN THE BLESSING LOOKS SO GOOD ON YOU!!

BEING THE AUTHENTIC YOU IS TO EXPENSIVE TO GIVE OUT DISCOUNTS

They Don't Know the COST of YOUR OIL!

Stand Tall

**Know who you are and
Never Be Afraid to
STAND UP FOR YOU**

Somewhere between child number 3 and 6 I gained what I considered to be a lot of weight. I was the heaviest I had ever been. I felt horrible for allowing myself to get to this point. I told myself it was ok, as long as I could still fit into my clothes. One day I went shopping and the size I convinced myself was ok, was too small. I stood in the fitting room at a loss for words. I could not believe I had crossed my own line, that I'd taken the time to draw in the *SAND*.

Now I had to decide. Would I take the time to lie to myself and say this next size was OK or would I DO something about it? I decided to do something about it and of course I went for all the quick weight loss plans first, 6 pills a day and my fat will go away......nah.... The LIES they tell!

One day I decided to go to a weight loss center. I walked in and of course I went to the wall of success and started visualizing myself being on the wall next (that is why they are there RIGHT).

The lady greets me with a smile and ask me to fill out paperwork. I hand it back to her with a corresponding smile. I'm excited because I anticipate a solution to my problem is near.

The next lady calls my name and greets me with a handshake and an automated smile. Let's break here for a moment and talk about my assessment of her smile. You see time is money and this lady doesn't know if I'll leave as a NEW member or walk out the door after I listen to her whole spiel and that's exactly how she acted.

We go into her office and she closes the door. She engages me in a conversation guided by the paperwork I've filled out (you know the one with all my naked truths on it). She proceeds by further undressing me, by asking me more questions that made me feel even lower than I did before I made the appointment. I was in the dressing room all over again.

After our conversation, she asked the question:
CAN I SIGN YOU UP?

The timing of this question was at what should have been my lowest point but something happened.

As I sat there counting the cost figuratively and literally, I decided I didn't want to spend the money and maybe I could try and do this on my own AGAIN. I shared my decision with her and then it got personal..........................

You see Ms. Lady started using all my naked truths I shared with her to help me, to now belittle me and pressure me into joining her team. It was one of the craziest experiences I had ever had. I kept asking myself is she really talking to ME? (this was pre-JESUS, you'll understand this better later).

I didn't like the size I was currently in BUT there wasn't anything traumatic that was going to happen if I didn't lose the weight. My husband wasn't bothered; my kids wasn't bothered. It didn't stop me from dressing nice or smelling good. It didn't make me stay at home. I WAS THE ONE WHO DIDN'T LIKE IT. Just like I didn't like the way this conversation was going.

I smiled at the lady and told her it wasn't that serious and her psychology games wasn't going to work on me. This only angered her as she watched her commission slip through her hands. If she would have spent more time building a bridge of understanding instead of a one-way pass to loserville, WE MAY HAVE BEEN ABLE TO WORK TOGETHER.

NEVER STOP KNOWING WHO YOU ARE. NO MATTER WHAT PEOPLE SAY ABOUT YOU, EVEN IF WHAT THEY ARE SAYING IS TRUE. You have the POWER to change. I was overweight by MY personal standards but I didn't have to stay that way. I had the power to change it AND I DID!

STAND IN YOUR TRUTH, WHILE KNOWING THAT YOU HAVE EVERYTHING IT TAKES TO MAKE THE NECESSARY ADJUSTMENTS.

People who make you feel small CAN NOT assist you in
FEELING TALL.

STOP ASKING OTHERS TO

LOVE

WHAT YOU DON'T EVEN LIKE

Fall in LOVE with ALL of you

Accept ALL of you

And BE WILLING to change what needs to be changed.

~Cynthia Essex

ULTIMATELY

The

CHOICE

WILL

ALWAYS

BE YOURS

Big Picture……. Blaming others undermines PERSONAL GROWTH

I've Hurt People

Ignorance is no Excuse!
No ifs, ands or buts.
You must deal with
our own PAIN or you
will always be a tool
to hurt others.

We always remember what others did to us, but how about what you did?

Somewhere is this book is a quote that says "Hurt People, Hurt People".

Weellllll let's talk about *that*. You can hurt someone so bad that there is no bouncing back from it (for them). They may forgive you so they can move on and be FREE but often times PEOPLE don't FORGET how you made them feel.

I was one of those hurt people walking around with no understanding of how this was impacting EVERYONE I was connected to. Ok let's go one step deeper. I hadn't thought to consider anyone but me, myself and I. I had no problem putting my foolery on display for all to see. Make me mad or mess with my FAMILY and you'd get the CYNTHIA ESSEX, HURT THEM AND LEAVE THEM TO DIE SHOW………. with a DROP THE MIC MOMENT! And I NEVER CARED how the other person felt. I was *committed* to making everyone pay for the hurt I was feeling (at that time, I didn't know that was what it was, I just knew it was temporarily satisfying)

If you ever encountered me in that state………YOU NEVER WILL FORGOT ME. It was sooo bad. The sad part for me was I may have done some damage way back then, that sent someone away from me deeply hurt and I never had an opportunity to apologize.

I had no idea Vengeance belonged to the LORD because the way my life was set up, that was my very **bestest** friend.

Here I am YEARS later with a renewed mind and an awareness of accountability for what I say and do. I no longer use my words to hurt people (I am honest and sometimes direct) but I'm not intentionally nasty. I work hard to stay away from people and situations that try to breathe new life into those old parts of me. Now, I don't run from a fight, I just fight different and I value the person over the win. I'm consistently in a state of ask myself:

1. How will this affect our relationship?
2. Is this person worth this fight?
3. In the long run, will this matter?
4. Is this person essential to my destiny?
5. Are my actions pleasing to God?

I LOVE THAT GOD LOVED ME ENOUGH NOT TO GIVE UP ON ME, SO I TRY TO MAKE PEOPLE A PRIORITY AND NOT GIVE UP ON THEM.

On my road to redemption I became somewhat of a push over (hard to believe RIGHT). I thought this is what the Christian LIFE was all about. I let people get away with things that would have been a major problem pre-JESUS.

First, I was waaaay left and then I went waaaayyy right and Today I'm confidently working towards the middle. If you read the story in this book titled "Storms" this was one of the benefits of going through that trying time. I got my **stance** back. Thank God!! I was really tired of bending over (take that however you'd like).

Whenever I have the opportunity to share this story I do. People hardly every believe me. I share this with people because I want them to know that people are not always intentional with the words they speak. They just don't know how to give pain another sound. They are stuck there and nobody is willing to go into the dark place and pull them out, especially if they have witnessed or heard about the *shows*.

NOW when people experience me is this state, they don't forget me.
What the enemy meant for bad, GOD has turned it for my good.

I'm not PERFECT but I'm working on it daily.
If I have hurt you, in any way PLEASE FORGIVE ME!

You Should Leave People
BETTER
off than you found them
#Goals

NO, I'm not like you

**But don't you
Laugh just yet**

Have you ever been told you don't fit in, that you are kooky, weird, or strange? Or maybe you were treated like you did not belong?

Welcome to the club!! You were not created to be like anyone else. You were created to look like you, dress like you, talk like you and live like you. You are created to be YOU and ONLY YOU.

It took me a long time to accept some of the things about me that were different, partly because I didn't have anyone around me that gave me permission to be me or who *consistently* modeled for me "different" being OK.

I remember sharing with my grandfather that kids were teasing me, about my lips being too big. HIS RESPONSE, will always be with me and it silenced the negative voices of then and it's applicable now.

He told me over and over that my lips were beautiful and someday women will pay for what God gave me. He was a WISE MAN and he was right, booty and lips seem to be hot commodities today. I won't even address the latter…… (laughing out loud…..I'm Blessed). He told me not to ever cover them up with lipstick, just shine them up with a little gloss and they'll be fine.

   Consider it not strange, mean or offensive when people tell you that they see your AUTHENTICITY in unintelligent ways.

        People FEAR what they don't
UNDERSTAND

        ACCEPT it, it is GODS BEAUTIFUL
           signature on you.

Once you understand it, you'll be able to walk in it.
FREE people, can FREE people.

Learning to BE confident with the skin, you are in is a part of
the journey of STANDING TALL.
Trust me, there is
NOTHING WRONG WITH YOU

The person who follows the crowd usually goes no further than the crowd. The person who walks alone is likely to himself in places no one has ever seen before.

-Albert Einstein

Maybe you feel like you
don't fit here

that's because you
didn't come from here

YOU ARE FROM
THE MIND OF CHRIST
That Right There is Why
YOU are so AMAZING

Who Is that?

They look so familiar

Are you ready for God to re-present you to the world? If not, get ready.

You thought this was the end of the story and life could not get any worse. You thought you had lived you best life…. BUT IT AIN'T OVER.

Don't become too comfortable with what it is, because what it is ain't what it's going to be!!

You didn't know a crack head could own a rehab center. You thought your life was over because you had drugs in your past.

You didn't know that a domestic violence survivor could minster to women about how she got out and started a business helping women.

You didn't know that, that drug dealing son, could open a youth center and counsel troubled youth.

You didn't know a high school dropout could go to college and Later hold the title of DR.

You didn't know what the doctors told you was impossible, was very possible.

You didn't know that you could survive a broken home and then be in a loving relationship.

You didn't know, when you dropped out of college to have your baby, that you could raise COLLEGE GRADUATES
You didn't know that dropping out of school, couldn't stop you from becoming a Successful Business Man.

You didn't know that your mute child could grow up and be a poet.

You didn't know that your latter would be greater.

I didn't know that this teen mom could

INSPIRE PEOPLE TO LIVE THEIR DREAMS
ENCOURAGE THE HOPELESS TO HAVE HOPE
USE HER LIFE TO TESTIFY TO THE GOODNESS OF
GOD

I LEARNED TO STAND TALL WHEN BEING SMALL
IS ALL I KNEW

I HOPE YOU ARE READY, GOD IS GOING TO
RE-PRESENT YOU TO THE WORLD. THEY DIDN'T
KNOW HE SPECAILIZES IN MAKING A MESS
MAGNIFICICANT.

So, don't be surprised when they whisper
IS THAT MARY'S BOY? (read yo bible)
THEY AIN'T KNOW

(Yes, I know I'm yelling again)

NEXT

You've already won this fight!

Lift your
Glass
for the
toast!

People are comfortable with you *talking* dreams, but they become kind of strange, when you doing your dream work, AND THEY BECOME INVISIBLE when your dreams have become a reality...................

Don't find it strange that the old group left you, they were supposed to. Why would you expect closed minds to be open to you dreaming BIG, when they are satisfied with the status quo?

When you think higher, you'll go higher and when you go higher, others will suddenly become uncomfortable with you.... You're one of "them" now they'll say. "Oooh you too good for us now". Don't be surprised by people who can't handle the NEW in you.

Don't hold yourself hostage to the limits others have placed on themselves and indirectly placed on you by association.

Group failing ain't cute! Now group success can be gorgeous......BUT YOU CAN'T WAIT FOR THEM (you can still support them, but not at the cost of delaying your dreams). You may have to unlock hands and be willing to move to a different circle OR you may have to stand alone in the NEW ROOM temporarily. (Don't' get it twisted, there's a cost associated with that place too)

Alone isn't a lonely place, it's the place where you grow, it's the place you see clearer, it's in THIS place you'll forever be LEARNING to STAND TALL.

Learn to lift your GLASS and toast yourself, because your supporting cast is subject to change..........

Don't let that concern you. Just look up and say

WHAT'S NEXT

"Getting to the TOP is only half the battle. The other half, is dealing with the people that think you left them behind"

~Charles Robinson

Here are Some Questions to Ponder

What are the things in your LIFE you enjoy doing, that you can't EVER see yourself *not* doing?

Do IT!! Follow Your Passions

Can you find a way to build people up, when tearing them down is all you know?

Can you Pursue Peace, even when your *RIGHT?*

Can you just let it go......this time?

Let your response, be the beginning of GROWTH

Is your TIME valuable to you or do you live your life, like you have an endless supply of it?

Can people be more important than position, when you're climbing the ladder of Success?

Define What Love Means To You

What
parts
of
you,
have
you
ignored?

What

Can

You

Do

NOW,

To

Change

your

Tomorrow?

YOU EVER SEE A REALLY UGLY GUY
WITH A BEAUTIFUL WOMAN
AND
YOU THINK TO YOURSELD
 HOW'D HE DO THAT?

HE MUST BE **REALLY FUNNY**

(DON'T JUDGE ME, I AM NOT ALONE IN THIS,
YOU'VE THOUGHT IT TOOOOO)

I had to have one random thing (just *petty*)

Why envy, when you can admire?

admire
regard (an object, quality, or person) with respect or warm approval.

Admire the grind, effort and courage it takes for people to BE whatever they want to be, to DO whatever they want to do and to HAVE whatever they want to have. Admiration says you appreciate the uniqueness of who they are. Take every opportunity to learn what principles they used to get what they have.

Once you have the principles, ask GOD for the plan.

envy
a feeling of discontented or resentful longing aroused by someone else's possessions, qualities, or luck.

The plan he gives you will keep you away from this emotion called envy, so will hard work and confidence. Don't allow envy to destroy you. Do all you can to stay away from that emotion called envy. Envy is stupid because it adds nothing to. Envy will leave you broke, busted and disgusted.

You have no idea what it cost to be someone else so just be content – BEING YOU.

Remember everything you see, ain't always what it be.

~Google.com

How do I

hold on to ME

And let go of

You

AT THE SAME TIME?

I HOLD ME A LITTLE TIGHTER

If you give away all you have,
to everyone else

what will you have left to give

TO YOU?

When will YOU be READY to STAND TALL?

It'll NEVER be CONVENIENT!

INSPIRATION

When you have a chance
Affirm
People never forget how you made them feel

Remember who you are:
Be strong and true to yourself **without** apology.

~Mary Walk

Check Yourself

Your LIFE's trouble ain't always
someone else's fault!

and
even
if it was
YOU have the POWER to CHANGE IT AND
THAT'S YOUR
RESPONDSIBITY

~Cynthia Essex

Your ability to BELIEVE
DETERMINES
Your ability to ACHIEVE
~Cierra Miller

Make Decisions that reflect your FAITH in GOD

NOT your fear of failure

~Jessica Patman

ALL NEGATIVITY

Keep it moving to the LEFT

Because you ain't RIGHT

~Cynthia Essex

BUT

Negates everything you said before it

use it wisely

Sometimes you must simply

walk away

And Leave it ALL Behind

~Cynthia Essex

I had to step OUT of my COMFORT ZONE to step INTO MY DESTINY

~Val Jackson

YOU

were created for a Purpose.
This is Certain.
Not debatable.
You are not here by chance.
You are here on purpose, for a purpose.
Should you choose to accept-that is left up to YOU.
~Jacquetta Dantzler

To Discover you
is TO DISCOVER
GREATNESS

~LaToya Peoples

Maybe it was Forgivable

BUT

NOT FORGETABLE

A simple Apology will not always be enough
Lessons Learned

~Cynthia Essex

Be An Original

Copies are cheap

DREAMING

IS

EASY

Anyone Can Do It

Commitment to see it come to pass is the SEPARATOR

APPRECIATION
is
APPRECIATED

It's better to do something and be bad at that,

    than to do nothing and be GREAT at that.

~Cynthia Essex

You can't be who you want to be

And

Who you are called to be

At the same time

Man, talk about confusion

~Cynthia Essex

Exposure

Expands

YOUR Perspective

Go, See, Do

~Cynthia Essex

Taking multiple small steps
is better than taking one

HUGE

STEP

then standing still

~Cynthia Essex

Getting what you WANT

may not always

be better than

getting what you NEED

~Cynthia Essex

If the milk spills more than twice
in a day,
stop pouring it

You my friend are probably tired.

Don't be PARALYZED by BROKENESS

Everything and Everybody Breaks At Some Point

~Cynthia Essex

I know it won't look like it and it certainly won't FEEL like it
BUT WHOLENESS FOLLOWS

Don't expect a Turtle to have a Giraffe's Perspective

-Bishop T.D. Jakes
The Potters House

Please don't

TAKE

more than you are willing to

DEPOSIT

Love Banks Can Run Low

~Cynthia Essex

Knowing you mattered to

one person

Makes life worth living

You Never Know Who's WATCHING

~Cynthia Essex

Start over as many

times as

you need to.
Just take the previous lessons with you
AND
remember LIFE DOESN'T HAPPEN IN A STRAIGHT LINE.

~Cynthia Essex

Wake up and expect the day to be GREAT

And It Will Be

~Cynthia Essex

No one can steal your shine,

only you can dull it!
Attitude is Everything

~Cynthia Essex

Don't just walk a mile

in her shoes

Spend a DAY in HER LIFE

~Cynthia Essex

When God Sets you FREE

DON'T

Go Back to being bound

Everything and Everyone you need is or will be with you

~Cynthia Essex

Stop Expecting
Orange Juice

from Apples

They Are Who They Are and you can't change that

~Cynthia Essex

DEATH is to be ABSENT FROM..................

So, CHOOSING not to be PRESENT in....

IS DEADLY

~Cynthia Essex

The Love Letters

Dear Past
Dear Present
Dear Future
Dear Husband
Dear Children
Dear God

**Take the time to write letters to your PAST,
PRESENT AND FUTURE.**
Accept what was
Live in what is
And GET EXCITED about what's coming

Dear Past

You and I have been together FOREVER. I'll admit sometimes I stayed in your presence to long. I couldn't help it. You're so fascinating. I didn't know it then but You hold the testimonies of my tomorrow.

You are the holder of my mistakes *but you also hold my accomplishments*. You have taught me so much and I appreciate you. You rarely get the proper credit because sometimes I referenced you in the wrong way. I didn't take the time to honor your gift of perspective. Your depth is immeasurable and I'm always learning something new from you.

I apologize for thinking you came to take, when the reality is you only came to give.

I thought this could be a break up letter but without you I could have never found my strength. Without your point of reference, I may have made unnecessary returns to people, places and things. Without you I may not have been able to push myself into victory one more time.

I LOVE the way you've taught me to have no regrets
I LOVE the LESSONS you are continually giving
I LOVE the way people receive the lessons you have taught

I LOVE THE WAY YOU HAVE ASSISTED ME IN
LEARNING TO STAND TALL

DEAR PRESENT

I LOVE being with you. You possess so much insight. You show off the best parts of me. You get me. You've allowed me to BE! And because you've made my past relevant, you've allowed me to live in this moment without fear or regret.

Thank you for partnering with my past to make me better. Thank you for your contributions of WISDOM to the newest parts of my past. Thank you for waking up in me each morning with a brand-new portion of grace and mercy (Lord knows I need it). I appreciate your check and balance system. You never allow me to get overwhelmed with tomorrows cares.

Thank you for the GIFT of TODAY

Thank You for presenting me with new opportunities of growth. Your commitment to living life in this moment is so peaceful and calming for me. Your patience with me is PERFECT. Thank you for believing in me and preparing me for my FUTURE.

Thank you for teaching me to LIVE within you. Thank you for teaching me the value of time. Thank you for helping me realize TODAY is all I have.

Thank you for assisting me in
LEARNING TO STAND TALL

DEAR FUTURE

My voice may sound familiar to you; I've been speaking into you for a long time. Sometimes it may have sounded strong and confident and sometimes it may have sounded unsure and scared. TODAY it sounds SURER and more confident than yesterday.

I know we'll be great together, because my *past* helped me to hope for you and the *present* continually painted vivid pictures of expectation. And although I've prepared to meet you, I have a strong feeling I won't be able to recognize you because you'll be bigger and better than anything my past could have seen for me.

I have invested time with you. I have denounced all the negative things that others said about you to me. I have spoken POWERFUL words to you about you. I want you to know that the *present* told me to keep speaking into you because "I'll have what I have said". I want to be honest with you, some of the things I said in my *past* showed up in my *present* and not all of those things were good. But I'll continually run toward you without fear or limitations. I won't allow the Adversities of LIFE to stop me from having all that YOU HAVE PREPARED FOR ME! I've learned the lessons of my past and I now KNOW THAT I have the POWER to DECLARE A NEW THING and IT WILL BE SO.

Thank you, FUTURE, for allowing me to
Learn to Stand even TALLER

DEAR HUSBAND

Thank you for being willing to ride this roller coaster of life with me. It truly has been a JOURNEY. Thank you for forcing me to look at me, when it was easier to look at you. Thank you for believing that I can do anything that I have had the courage to share with you.

Thank you for giving me your time, your talent and your treasure. Thank you for keeping the power on. Thank you for provision. Thank you for being an example to our children and all the children that came with them, we are true villagers.

Thank you for the late-night donut runs

Thank you for being a good son, and assuring we'll have an abundance of time together. Thank you for serving an unfailing GOD. Thank you for Praying for our children and believing God for the best to be present in OUR lives. Thank you for staying when leaving is always an option.

Thank you for seeing the best parts of me.... I KNOW IT WASN'T ALWAYS EASY.

Thank you for supporting my stumbling
WHILE I was

LEARNING TO STAND TALL

TO MY BABIES
THANK YOOOUU
(Yes I'm YELLING)

To my eldest daughter THANK YOU for allowing me to grow up with you.

Thank you to all my babies, YOU'VE MADE ME BETTER! Our challenges have not been in vain. We have learned, grown, supported and LOVED each other past some hard days AND WE'RE STILL STANDING.

PLEASE KNOW THAT I LOVE YOU TODAY, YESTURDAY AND FOREVER

You are the reasons I am continually in pursuit of
LEARNING TO STAND TALL

I wasn't a PERFECT MOM but I've ALWAYS HAD YOUR PURPOSES ON MY MIND

DEAR GOD

I am soooo grateful for EVERYTHING that you have done and are doing in my life.

I know that I disagreed with ~~some~~ most of your tactics. I didn't TRULY understand that YOU KNEW WHAT WAS BEST FOR ME.

Thank you for always being PRESENT in my LIFE. Thank you for allowing me to come into the knowledge of who you are in me.

Thank you for THINKING OF ME.

Thank you for SAVING ME (literally) repeatedly.

Thank you for the hedge of protection you placed around me, when I was not strong enough to help myself.

Thank you for DWELLING within me.

THANK YOU FOR TEACHING ME LIFE LESSONS IN WAYS THAT ONLY YOU CAN.

THANK YOU FOR BEING GOD
THANK FOR ALLOWING YOUR SON TO DIE FOR ME

THANK YOU FOR LOVING ME ENOUGH TO SACRAFICE YOUR LIFE. I'M FOREVER INDEBTED TO YOU, YOU HAVE ALLOWED ME TO

STAND TALL

Distraction come To distract
you

From reaching your full potential
in any given situation

Some of them **look** like answers to prayers you've prayed

~Cynthia Essex

People like to reference your past

WHEN YOUR FUTURE

IS BRIGHT!

Don't Be Bothered. Get some SEXY SHADES!

~Cynthia Essex

God has an
AMAZING PLAN
FOR YOUR
LIFE

Can you accept that?

Though I may fail
                    miserably

from time to time.

I will never tire of trying to
BE and DO BETTER

~Charlene Orange

A single decision can have a DOMINO EFFECT

Think FIRST

~Cynthia Essex

NEVER
FORGET
WHO
YOU
ARE ....

BECAUSE
YOU
BAD Gurl!

Girl You B.A.D

BRANDED and DISTINGUISHED

You've been uniquely created, Spoken into existence by the CREATOR himself. Set apart, Girted and Pre-ordained for Success.

BAFFLING and DELIGHTFUL

No one knows HOW you do what you do, when you have so much to do So Beautifully

BLUNT and DAUNTLESS

You are HONEST and DIRECT. You always mean what you say and say what you mean. You are not afraid to speak up for who or what is RIGHT.

BOUNTIFUL and DESERVING

Because GIVING is you LIFESTYLE, you are abundantly BLESSED. You lack Nothing and your Worthy of GOD'S BEST.... DON'T EVER FORGET THAT

BRILLANT AND DEMANDING

You have Million Dollar thoughts consistently flowing through your head and YOU speak the WORD FAITHFULLY reminding GOD of what he said!

Oh, Did I tell you, YOU BAD GIRL

~Cynthia Essex

BUOYANT and DIGNIFIED

No matter what labels you wear you keeps it all together, CLASSY, CKEAN AND COLLECTED. YOU always look like a WINNER.

BURGEONING and DETERMINED

You are always self-evaluating and seeking way to grow, your committed to CHANGE, not just for you but for everyone you know.

BOLD and DELIBERATE

You are FEARLESS (take that in) KNOWING the one who lives in you has ordered every step.... YES, even the ones you thought were mistakes. He's so INTENTIONAL.... NOTHING can be wasted, he'll use every ache.

BUILDER and DEFINER

You have stood on EVERY brick thrown you way, it may have caused you to stumble BUT LOOK AT YOU TODAY.

WE ARE BIG VISIONARIES AND WE ARE DIVERSE

We come in all shapes and shades and with luggage of many colors in tow, but we come together to support, love and help one another GROW.

I JUST THOUGHT I'D LET YOU KNOW

GIRL YOU B.A.D

~Cynthia Essex

A MESSAGE FROM **DR. SHAREASE PRICE**

To the Readers

The way God has used Cynthia in this text is guaranteed to be a wind of freshness and rejuvenation to your life. In these times, with women insecurities at an all-time high, the transparency she delivers is extremely hard to find and so desperately needed. Her nakedness and failures she shares is the epitome of how God will truly take your ashes and transform them into beauty. Therefore, I can never foresee you sitting down on "you" anymore after sincerely grabbing and receiving this game changing book.

To Cynthia

Your presence alone is electrifying and transforming, so I cannot completely fathom the depth of how your God breathed words in this book will impact! I am so Godly proud of you for standing tall and fighting to become the woman you are at this very moment. Your shared journey is an array of hope, and that is exactly what we all need today. So, for those who may never thank you personally for persevering through the pressure and temptation of aborting the process of completing this God assigned book, I say: "thank you". Freedom to be is contagious, so be proud of the guaranteed lives God will touch because you have decided to continuously fight to "Stand Tall". I love you, and as always, Keep Dominating!

This woman is A POWERHOUSE. I LOVE her beyond words. Thank you for seeing God's Masterpiece buried in my pain. Thank you for BEING YOU!

~Cynthia Essex

Credits and Special Acknowledgements

Front Cover: Shaun Bangert (Thank you for your **insight**)
Back Cover: Christopher Essex

Inspirations in the Book: My Family and Friends

My Dream Keepers (they wouldn't let me quit)
      Pastors Tariq and ShaRease Price
      Mr. Levi C. Essex
      Jacquetta Dantzler
      Jessica Patman
      Margo Cirilo
      Loyce Seals-Brown
      LaToya Peoples
      Jamie Garcia
      Dr. Charles Green IV
      -THANK YOU for CONSTANTLY HARRASSING ME, I
      would not have finished this book without YOU

      Drs Ron and Georgette Frierson
      -Thank You for giving me a STRONG FONDATION

Bible Scriptures Referenced
NIV
King James
Message
New Living Translation

THANK YOU for believing in me enough to
STAND TALL WITH ME

WELCOME TO THE BEGINNING

#SheREADY